EFFECTIVE PLANNING STRATEGIES AND PROPOSAL WRITING

A Workbook for Helping Professionals

Salene J. Cowher

Larry S. Dickson

University Press of America,® Inc.
Lanham · Boulder · New York · Toronto · Plymouth, UK

Copyright © 2010 by
University Press of America,® Inc.
4501 Forbes Boulevard
Suite 200
Lanham, Maryland 20706
UPA Acquisitions Department (301) 459-3366

Estover Road
Plymouth PL6 7PY
United Kingdom

Library of Congress Control Number: 2009938780
ISBN: 978-0-7618-4976-6 (paperback : alk. paper)
eISBN: 978-0-7618-4977-3

For all of the wonderful graduate students I've had the privilege of teaching during the past 17 years; also my wonderful family.

Contents

Preface

For the past 17 years, Salene Cowher, Ph.D., N.C.C., L.P.C., has taught graduate students at Edinboro University of Pennsylvania, Edinboro, PA. As a professor with specialization in counselor education, Dr. Cowher has taught counseling courses that included research methods and planning. She has also written extensively on topics related to counseling theory and practice. Dr. Cowher has also maintained a private practice, working with individuals, couples, families, and those seeking consultation and supervision.

This text reflects several years of work, beginning with efforts that manifested in an earlier edited publication that included articles recommended by Dr. Cowher's graduate students. Work began in earnest toward the present publication when a former student, co-author Larry Dickson, agreed to assist in augmenting and editing the text. Former student, Danielle Prester, was additionally helpful in editing and processing the material.

Acknowledgments

Special thanks go to Ms. Danielle Prester for her fine work on the text. Without her efforts, the finished product would not be possible. Her insights as a former student were also invaluable.

Thanks, too, to Mr. Ed Sitter, Director of Planning and Program Development for the Greater Erie Community Action Committee in Erie, Pennsylvania. His willingness to share information and work with graduate students is commendable.

Thanks to Ms. Marie Beiswenger, secretary, for her assistance with duplication, copying, and etc., as well to the graduate students from my planning classes who used various drafts of the text and provided feedback.

Thanks to family members who are only too aware of the time and effort required to complete a writing project.

Finally, thanks to Ms. Samantha Kirk from University Press for being patient with us on the effort.

Chapter 1
Overview of Proposals

Chapter Outcomes: At the completion of this chapter, activities and assignments, the student will:

1. Identify and describe the components of a planning document (proposal).
2. Identify Change Model Steps
3. Understand the concepts of "planned change"
4. Understand the concepts of goals and objectives in a planning document
5. Develop Change Opportunity ideas
6. Develop preliminary Change Opportunity Work Statements

Overview:

There is no mystery to developing a successful Change Model. The process involves following these identified Change Model Steps:

1. Identify the opportunity
2. Analyze the opportunity (gather information for rationale/need)
3. Set goals and objectives
4. Design and structure the effort
5. Develop the resource plan
6. Implement the effort
7. Monitor the change effort (formative evaluation)
8. Evaluate the final result(s) (summative evaluation)
9. Reassess and stabilize the situation (re-decide)

In addition, the change agent needs to ensure that the funding source is thoroughly researched, that a strong relationship is built with the funders, and that the proposal is written according to the funders' specifications.

Quintessence: "Typical" components of planning document (proposal):

1. *Introduction* to opportunity: hits most salient points very quickly, with reference to *design structures*, and *funding level* (if applicable). Brief reference is frequently made to the *change agent* and his/her qualifications, as well. Some funding sources insist that the change agent include a copy of his/her résumé in the appendices. Should this be the case, the change agent may make a reference to the appendix where the resume is included. This component is generally about one page in length.
2. *Rationale:* includes localized *need assessment data* (if available) and a review of *literature*. Literature included should be current and applicable to the opportunity. Often, two subheadings will be used in this section, i.e. Needs Assessment and Related Literature. Anything that is particularly unique to this initiative, especially compared to similar ones elsewhere, should be justified in the Rationale. The length of this section can vary. In general, it is probably 3-5 pages long.
3. *Needs Assessments* conducted for planning purposes should reflect the needs of potential consumers. These are used to assess whether or not the efforts should move forward. Often, needs assessment instruments can be used, in part, as the basis for evaluation instruments used once the effort is in place. Needs assessments can be written or in verbal

(interview) format. Some change agents may provide both written and interview (follow-up to written) formats. Some change agents use written, survey formats. Surveys should be brief, concise, and understandable to the surveyed population. Likert scale formats are frequently used. Mailed surveys should include self-addressed, stamped envelopes for replies. Marginally, a 10% response from the target population is considered significant. It is always recommended that surveys be piloted with individual(s) similar to the target population but not likely to actually participate.

      a. "Need" is frequently broken-down into three categories: *Perceived Need, Expressed Need, and Relative Need*. Most needs assessments reflect Expressed and/or Perceived Need, although some change agents attempt to provide data from all three. Additionally need can be expressed as Normative Need. These types of need are defined as follows:

            i. *Perceived Need:* determined by surveying service providers to target population
            ii. *Expressed Need:* determined by surveying actual members of the target population
            iii. *Relative Need:* determined by comparing your locality, agency, etc. or with others that are similar, i.e. Erie Metropolitan area being compared to Scranton Metropolitan area. If Scranton is similar in size, etc. to Erie and is providing a service that Erie is not, then the change agent could profess *Relative Need.*

    4. The change agent should identify the category (ies) of Need(s) being described.

EXAMPLE:

Bethesda Children's Home is requesting $20,000.00 in HSDF (Human Services Development Funds), as part of the total start up budget of $30,000.00 for the L.E.A.P. Scholarship Program (Let Everyone Actively Participate). These HSDF monies along with matching funds from the Bethesda Foundation will be utilized for foster-children's participation in strengths based Arts, athletics, and structured recreational/educational activities.

Identification of Need

A needs assessment was presented to 42 Crawford County children and adolescents participating in Bethesda's Foster-Care program to assess **expressed need**. A Children's Activity Questionnaire was made available for voluntary completion between April 1, 2004 and April 8, 2004. In addition **expressed need** was also assessed through structured interviews with six foster-care children whose ages ranged from under five to eighteen years old.

Perceived need has been demonstrated through a voluntary Foster Parent Questionnaire completed by forty-six Crawford County foster parents and through structured interviews with six foster-care parents. In addition, **perceived need** was demonstrated by individual letters of need and support from three foster-care families currently living in Crawford County.

Relative need Despite shrinking resources, communities across the country have developed programs to teach young people new ways to acquire personal power and self-discipline and to engage the youth constructively in their community. These programs are successful because they link individual artist, coaches, musicians, skilled athletes, scholars, and organizational leaders with at risk youth; in strengths based programs. These programs offer an alternative for success and respectability for children and adolescents in areas of education, self-esteem, improved communication and socialization, development of coping skills, improved problem solving skills, increased employability, and a sense of belonging to a group or community. For a comparison to this grant proposal, the following is a small sampling of successful programs for youth: The Mitte Foundation, Cultural Giving Program 6836 Bee Caves Road, Suite 262 Austin, TX 78746 www.mittefoundation.org/cultural/guidelines.html; The Boys Choir of Harlem 2005 Madison Avenue New York, NY 10035 Phone: 212-289-1815; Children of the Future, Greater Columbus Arts Council 55 East State Street Columbus, OH 43215 Phone: 614-224-2606; The Youth Services League, Projects and Activities 2323 East 21ˢᵗ Street Brooklyn, NY 11229 Phone: 71646-5613; and Pittsburgh Center for the Arts 1047 Shady Avenue Pittsburgh, PA 5232 Phone: 412-361-0455.

---

1. *Goals and Objectives:* usually provided in a listing format. This section may also include activities related to each objective. *Goals* refer to the change agent's vision for the effort and are generally too broad to be measurable. Since these are the change agent's "dreams" for the future, there should only be 1-3 Goals. Objectives are tangible steps toward the potential attainment of the Goals.

Objectives are frequently used by external reviewers after the completion of a change effort to assess the effectiveness of the endeavor. Therefore, objectives should be written concisely and effectively, each one including the following elements: the *target population,* the *direction of the intended change,* a *time frame,* and a *measurable criterion* that provides evidence of success. The Evaluation Plan should evidence a direct connection to the Objectives.

EXAMPLE:

Sample Goal and Related Objectives:

Goal I. to enhance the self-esteem of single parents

    Objective IA: to provide testing services to all single parents enrolled in the fall, 2009 Cowher Self-Esteem Improvement Program

    Objective IB: to utilize test results in providing individual counseling sessions for all single parents enrolled in the fall, 2009 Cowher Self-Esteem Improvement Program

    Objective IC: to conduct post-testing with all single parents enrolled in the fall, 2009 Cowher Self-Esteem Improvement Program that reflects a 50% increase in self-esteem

Discussion: Note breadth of Goal. Also note the elements included with each. *Objective. IA:* direction of intended change = to provide testing services; time frame = fall, 2009; target population = single parents enrolled in Cowher Self-Esteem Improvement Program; measurable criterion = all (single parents)

Objective. IB: direction of intended change = to utilize test results in providing individual counseling sessions; time fall = fall, 2009; target population = single parents enrolled in Cowher Self-Esteem Improvement Program; measurable criterion = all (single parents)

Objective. IC: direction of intended change = to conduct post-testing that reflects an increase in self-esteem; time frame = fall, 2009; target population = single parents enrolled in Cowher Self-Esteem Improvement Program; measurable criteria = all (single parents) & 50% increase in self-esteem (according to post-tests).

Each Goal should have at least two Objectives. This section is typically no more than 2-3 pages in length.

2.   *Methods:* includes brief discussion of *Design* (project, program, policy, combination) and *Action Plan* (Activities). Activities will frequently be formatted with the related Objective. Gantt charts, which are used to reflect time frames for completion of Activities, are often included without need for any narrative.

    3 Types of Change Effort Designs:

        a.   *Program Design* – lasting @ least 6 months w/ provisions of direct service to consumers

        b.   *Policy Change Design* – change in organizational structure or adding a position

        c.   *Project Design* – short term, usually less than 6 months that a project is completed or accomplished

EXAMPLES:

Objective IA: to provide testing services to all single parents enrolled in the fall, 2009 Cowher Self-Esteem improvement Program

Date	Activity
7/09-8/09	Recruit parents for the program
	Order tests
	Send reminders to enrollees
	Make sure that tests and related materials have arrived
9/3/09	Welcome parents to the program
	Explain tomorrow's testing
	Make sure that testing materials and examiners are ready
9/4/09	Test enrollees
	Score tests

The length of this section varies, according to the configuration of Activities.

Activity	J	F	M	A	M	J	J	A
1. Identify potential client	■							
2. Interview and screen potential clients		■						
3. Select group participants			■					
4. Reserve a room and notify participants				■				
5. Make child-care arrangements				■				
6. Hold eight weekly meetings					■			
7. Collect and compile evaluation data					■	■	■	
8. Make recommendations to director								■

Activity	Person Responsible	Week Number 1	2	3	4	5	6	7	8	9	10	11	12
1. Get publicity on group program out to social service agencies, domestic violence shelters, police, and other resources to solicit applicants	Staff Member A	■	■	■	■	■	■	■	■	■			
2. Develop format for screening and assessment	Staff Member B	■	■	■									
3. Develop pretest and posttest	Staff Member B	■	■	■									
4. Develop information packet describing group program to give to women who have been through screening and assessment	Staff Member A			■	■								
5. Screen and assess at least 50 women for the program	Staff Member C				■	■	■	■	■	■	■	■	
6. Develop client-profile reports for group leaders	Staff Member B												■
7. Develop summary report for program director	Staff Member B												■

3. *Resource Plan:* should include ALL Resources necessary for change effort to take place. The resource plan is a project plan from a financial standpoint. Typical items to include in this financial perspective incorporate detailed itemized estimates of all expenditures and contribution from all sources, projected revenues, subtotals and totals, and the amount

and distribution of funds needed to perform the project activities over the allotted change episode. Specific areas include Personnel, Equipment, Space, Utilities, Materials, and Services. If a *Budget* is required, the general format is a zero-based, line-item budget. Such a budget presumes that no money has been carried over in any fashion from another endeavor, budget, etc. This budget is written Item-by-item, with "item" referring to a category of expenses. Typical items include: Personnel, Equipment, Space, Utilities, Materials, and Services. The Budget would include only those line items that are not being otherwise provided and only those items that the funding source will provide. Some funding sources, for example, will not fund equipment. Personnel line-items will typically be subdivided into Salaries and Benefits, with an itemized listing of costs for Benefits. Salaries at the level of the Personnel being requested and related Benefits costs are readily obtained through grants offices and personnel offices. ALL proposals include a Resource Plan, even if a Budget is not necessary.

4. Any item in the Budget that is atypical for efforts, such as yours, and/or especially costly should be explained in *Budget Notes*. Budget Notes are usually provided in a footnote form at the end of the Budget. Items that are described in Budget Notes usually have asterisks (*) placed at the end of their line on the Budget, with an accompanying asterisk (*) next to the Budget Note. Think of the format for footnotes, and you should understand this concept. Some funding sources will insist that costs be computed in Budget Notes or on the Budget line per item. For example, if you were budgeting for Duplicating service costs for $10.00, the funder might want you to note that this reflects 50 copies @ $.20 per copy. The funder might want this breakdown included on the Budget line, itself, or in a Budget Note. Justify the item, not the expense. The Resource Plan is typically no more than two pages long.

    a. *The Proposal Budget:* For many programs, the funding levels change annually. This is especially true of government programs that rely on budget appropriations from year to year. Once again, be realistic in your approach to budget preparation. Utilize a realistic inflation factor.

Salaries - Calculate salaries at anticipated rate at the start of project. Utilize an inflation factor to anticipate salary increases during the length of the project.

Fringe Benefits - If an internal rate is not determined, you will need to calculate a fringe benefits cost for each salary such as health insurance, social security, life insurance and workman's compensation.

Equipment - Obtain quotes where possible for equipment. Besides providing the most up to date information to the agency, this will provide a justification should additional information be requested.

Travel - For airline travel, obtain fare costs from the airlines to estimate the cost of the trip. Follow the internal guidelines on lodging, food and miscellaneous. Review funding agency guidelines to insure that travel supported though the grant is not reimbursed at government rates. If this is the case, then you may have to share some of the expenses and you need to plan accordingly.

Indirect Costs - If allowed by the agency, is generally a rate approved by a cognizant agency of the government for your agency. If you do not have an approved rate, you may have to negotiate with the agency to either obtain an approved rate or what items can be included in the calculation of your indirect costs. Some funding agencies place a cap on indirect costs and require the applicant to request only that designated percentage. Indirect costs generally include costs not directly assigned to the grant, such as heat, light, administrative costs, etc.

Matching Funds - As dollars available become tighter, many private and public agencies are requiring a commitment from applicants in the form of matching funds. Matching funds may be in the form of cash or in-kind. Cash will require that the applicant make available funds to pay for part of the cost of the program. In-kind funds may be in the form of facilities use, personnel time, materials and equipment use provided by the applicant. In-kind funds may also include indirect costs. Although indirect costs may not be permitted as part of the request from the funding agency, it may be permissible to include these costs as part of the match. Once again, it is important to carefully read the guidelines of the funding agency.

EXAMPLE #1:

Instructions: Applicant to insert entries on the "Proposed Expenditures" line under each appropriate heading (these figures are obtained from the attached detailed budgets).

Rounding Figures: All amounts must be rounded to the nearest dollar for budgeting purposes.

Secondary Institutions Only:
    To preclude duplicate reporting of local matching for instructional salaries ONLY, please indicate in the block below, the amount included in the proposed expenditures, local column, Instructional Salaries/Benefits, which also are being reported on the PDE 5023, Basic Data for District School Personnel.

$0 - (ALL applicants must complete this block; if not applicable, enter zero)

No Benefits

ITEMS	SHARE OF PROPOSED EXPENDITURES			TOTALS
	LOCAL	STATE	FEDERAL	
Instructional Salaries/Benefits				
Proposed Expenditures	0	0	0	0
Non-Instructional Salaries/Benefits				
Proposed Expenditures	0	0	$ 9,765.	$ 9,765.
Equipment				
Proposed Expenditures	0	0	0	0
Other (Include all items not identified above)				
Proposed Expenditures	0	0	$ 28,450.	$ 28,450.
TOTALS				
Total Proposed Expenditures	$ 1,529.	0	$ 38,215.	$ 39,744.
Total Approved Amounts				

Minimum non-federal support level   ____4____ %
                                        Total Non-Federal

EXAMPLE #2:

Resource Plan

Budget

The following is a list of project costs, listing all items that are necessary for the Property Acquisition for Expanded Parking Facilities Change Effort to take place.

Property Acquisition for Expanded Parking Facilities Change Effort	Grant Funds	Active Aging Foundation matching funds	Total
Purchase of property	$225,000.00		$225,000.00
Lot improvements [signage, curbing, drainage, and paving]	$50,000.00	$100,000.00	$150,000.00
Yearly increased operational costs [taxes, snow removal, greens upkeep & repairs]		$2,000.00	$2,000.00
Total for Budget	$275,000.00	$102,000.00	$377,000.00

Budget Narrative

Financial Supports and Grants Associated with Change Effort
While the purchase price for the property is $225,000.00, the total cost of the change effort is estimated to be $377,000.00. The City of Meadville Code requires a drainage system, curbing and paving at an additional cost of approximately $150,000.00. Completion of this change effort would minimally increase the operating expenses related to snow removal, taxes, greens upkeep, and repairs. Active Aging Inc. would budget approximately $2,000.00 annually from the general oper-

ating budget to cover these expenditures. While awaiting a decision on this grant, the Active Aging Inc. supporting foundation is beginning fundraising efforts to provide matching funds in the amount of $100,000.00 for the development of the property. In addition, the Senior Center will be asked to pledge an amount of approximately $5,000.00 to the change effort fund (XXXX, CEO, personal communication, June 12, 2009).

5. *Evaluation Plan:* should include *Formative* and *Summative* Evaluations. Usually, proposals will have subheadings for each of these categories of evaluation, with reference made to actual sample copies of the evaluation instruments included in the appendices. *Formative Evaluation* refers to evaluation being conducted throughout the change effort, while *Summative Evaluation* refers to evaluation conducted at the end of the effort. In discussing the Evaluation Plan, change agents should refer to the *instrumentation* to be used and *the format of that instrument*, i.e. participants will complete a 10-item survey instrument in Likert scale format, using a five-point scale, with 1 being lowest and 5 being highest. The Plan should also discuss the *statistics* to be used in compiling results, as well as *to who results will be disseminated.* In planning, we generally use statistics that are easily understood, such as basic measures of central tendency (mean, median, mode), percentages, etc.

Minimally, presenters, planning team members, supervisors, funding providers should receive results. Anyone involved in deciding about the future course of the effort should probably have access to the results; the funder should definitely get them. It is also very important that the change agent *note the criterion or criteria that will determine "success".* For example, if I am computing mean averages, using the Likert scale format just described, I may deem a mean average of 3.0 and anything above that as indicating "success". Summative Evaluation plans often include data from follow-up surveys (outcomes) over time. This section is usually about two pages in length.

EXAMPLE:

Formative Evaluation
Evaluation will be conducted throughout the change effort. The Planning team will meet monthly during the change effort implementation period. The members will meet in a focus group format, addressing issues, obstacles, and change effort progress.

Summative Evaluation
Evaluation will be conducted at the completion of the change effort. An evaluation assessment will be presented to a minimum of 200 individuals participating in activities or events at the Crawford County Community Center to assess the change effort completion. A Parking Survey Questionnaire will be made available for voluntary completion between January 1, 2009 and January 15, 2009 (See Appendix E). The Parking Survey Questionnaire consists of 10 questions. There are two forced answer questions related to persons with disabilities eligibility that require a yes/no response. A Likert scale is used to respond to 8 questions related to personal Crawford County Community Center usage and parking. An open-ended question is also included in the survey, soliciting suggestions for improvement of the parking conditions at the Crawford County Community Center. In addition, the change agent will also assess the change effort success through the completion of five structure interviews with senior citizens (See Appendix F). The criteria for the selection of the interviewees will include: voluntary participation, individuals 60 or older, participation in community center activities or events at least monthly, and two of the five individuals will have identified disabilities that would qualify them for a persons with disabilities placard. Data from these assessment instruments will be compared with the initial need assessment raw data collected in June of 2008. The results will be sent to the funding source and the Active Aging, Inc.

Criteria for Success
Success will be measured by the responses senior center consumers provide on the Evaluation Survey Questionnaires and information gathered during the five structured interviews. Projected summary samplings from these assessment instruments would include an increase in satisfaction rating with the overall parking facilities, and increased availability of convenient accessible persons with disabilities parking accommodations, and an increase of Community Center services and activities by the senior citizens. This change agent is looking for a 75% satisfaction rating with the parking facilities and persons with disabilities parking availability as a result of the completed change effort. If less than a 75% increase in satisfaction is indicated from the assessment tools, this change agent will consider the change effort unsuccessful.

---

6. *Reassessment and Stabilization:* at the end of a change effort or funding cycle, a final report is drafted. The final report follows the same format as described, written in the past tense. The report also includes a Reassessment and Stabilization section. This section provides a summary of the evaluative results from the perspective of the change agent and/or members of the planning team. It also provides reflection about "what worked" and "what didn't" and the future of the effort. The major questions addressed in this section are: Will we continue? Should we continue? Do we want to continue? How can we continue, if we want to? If we do continue, what should stay the same? If we do continue, what should change?

7. *Reference Listing & Appendices:* a Reference Listing that includes ONLY those references cited within the text should be included at the end of a proposal, unless the change agent wants to include a listing of References Consulted. In that case, a clear differentiation between the two types of References should be in evidence. Appendices should follow. Typical Appendices include: sample needs assessment instrument(s), sample evaluation instruments, sample modules (if used) and/or other sample materials (if needed), the change agent's resume (if required), resumes of key personnel (if needed), etc. Some funding sources are also beginning to solicit full proposals over the Internet.

Funding Sources may also want Appendices included that reflect certain Assurances that the agency is compliant with federal legislation regarding equal employment, nondiscrimination, etc. They may also ask for letters of support from community members, members of the target population, service providers, etc. and/or require that an advisory board or planning team be identified and noted.

EXAMPLE #1:

Sample Assurance

CONTRIBUTION TOWARD ECONOMIC INDEPENDENCE:

In October of 2007, CCAC, Allegheny initiated a pilot Single Parents and Homemaker Program called Program for Adults in Career Transition (PACT). As of May 6, 2008, program personnel had successfully assisted <u>43</u> participants in finding training programs relevant to their career goals at institutions, such as CCAC, Connelly Skills, Duff's Business Institute, Robert Morris, Learning Unlimited, and through JTPA.

Twenty participants successfully gained employment through PACT. Participants found the following positions:

Administrative Assistant(s)	Housekeeper(s)
Advertiser(s)	Landscaper(s)
Baker(s)	Sales Clerk(s)
Bookkeeper(s)	Secretary(ies)
Counter Manager(s)	Waitress(es)
Echo Cardiographer(s)	

The ever-increasing interest in the pilot program indicates the need for a new, more comprehensive training program for the 2007-08 funding year. This new training program would be geared specifically toward the needs of those program participants who have established career goals.

EXAMPLE #2:

Sample Assurance

CONTRIBUTION TOWARD ECONOMIC INDEPENDENCE:

In October 2007, CCAC, Allegheny initiated a pilot Single Parents and Homemaker Program called Program for Adults in Career Transition (PACT). As of May 6, 2008, program personnel had successfully assisted <u>43</u> participants in finding training programs relevant to their career goals at institutions, such as CCAC, Connelly Skills, Duff's Business Institute, Robert Morris, Learning Unlimited, and through JTPA.

Twenty participants successfully gained employment through PACT, finding positions as Sales Clerk, Administrative Assistants, Secretary, Echo Cardiographer, Counter Manager, Advertiser, Waitress, Bookkeeper, Housekeeper, Landscaper, and Baker. The ever-increasing interest in the pilot program indicates the need for a new, more comprehensive training program for the 2008-09 funding year. This new training program would be geared specifically toward the needs of those program participants who have established career goals.

TO DO!

1. Developing Change Opportunities Ideas
A.   Generate five new ideas to be developed.

   a. _____
       _____
       _____

   b. _____
       _____
       _____

   c. _____
       _____
       _____

   d. _____
       _____
       _____

   e. _____
       _____
       _____

B. Identify the unique qualities of each idea.

   a. _____
       _____
       _____

   b. _____
       _____
       _____

   c. _____
       _____
       _____

   d. _____
       _____
       _____

   e. _____
       _____
       _____

C. Identify who else may be doing this type of initiative. Is there a duplication of effort? If so, with whom? Is there a possi-
    bility for collaboration on this idea?

   a. _____
       _____
       _____

   b. _____
       _____
       _____

   c. _____
       _____
       _____

   d. _____
       _____
       _____

   e. _____
       _____
       _____

D. Identify the community need that is being met by each idea.

a. _____
    _____
    _____

b. _____
    _____
    _____

c. _____
    _____
    _____

d. _____
    _____
    _____

e. _____
    _____
    _____

E. Identify the community supports for each idea. (Include civic groups, political leaders, media, consumer groups, etc.)

a. _____
    _____
    _____

b. _____
    _____
    _____

c. _____
    _____
    _____

d. _____
    _____
    _____

e. _____
    _____
    _____

F. Identify available sources of expertise for each idea; indicating if the resource is internal or needs to be acquired from outside the organization.

Internal	Needs to be acquired

a. _____

b. _____

c. _____

d. _____

e. _____

G. Identify the existence of internal and external support for each idea.

Internal	External

a. _____

b. _____

c. _____

d. _____
    _____
e. _____
    _____

2. Review and discuss the five ideas and identify the best *Change Opportunity*.

Develop the statement of need by answering the question:
   What community need(s) does the idea address?
_____
_____
_____
_____

Develop the goals and objectives by answering the question:
   What would an enhanced community initiative look like?
_____
_____
_____
_____

Develop the methods by answering the question:
   What steps can be taken to enhance the current circumstances?
_____
_____
_____
_____

Develop the evaluation by answering the question:
   How will the success of the initiative be decided?
_____
_____
_____
_____

Develop the budget by answering the question:
   What will the cost be for this effort?
_____
_____
_____
_____

Develop the sustainability of the initiative by answering the question:
   How will the effort be funded in the future?
_____
_____
_____
_____

Key terms and Concepts: Can you define and explain each of the following key terms? Are you prepared to offer brief examples or applicable context for each concept?

Budget:
_____
_____

Change Agent:

_____

_____

Change Effort:

_____

_____

Expressed Need:

_____

_____

Formative Evaluation:

_____

_____

Needs Assessment:

_____

_____

Opportunity:

_____

_____

Perceived Need:

_____

_____

Proposal:

_____

_____

Relative Need:

_____

_____

Resource Plan:

_____

_____

RFP:

_____

_____

Summative Evaluation:

_____

_____

Questions:

Explain the difference between a goal and an objective.

What are the key components of an **objective**?

Chronicle and Rumination:

This is the space provided to *chronicle* your thoughts and to *ruminate* over the material presented in this chapter along with the references, outside readings, classroom activities, and experiences. Documenting your thoughts and feelings will provide a written account of your *Effective Planning Strategies and Proposal Writing* education.

Chapter 2
Analysis and Documentation of Need

Chapter Outcomes: At the completion of this chapter, activities and assignments, the student will:

1. Identify and define types of Change designs
2. Define variables effecting needs for planning
   a. Analyze a needs assessment
   b. Identify types of needs required in a proposal
3. Understand how to analyze a change opportunity.
   a. Determine why the opportunity exists and define its aspects and implications
   b. Identify technical aspects of the change opportunity: etiology, theory, research
   c. Identify interpersonal aspects of the change opportunity
   d. Analyze the force field surrounding the change opportunity
4. Understand and demonstrate the use of a SWOT in strategic planning process

Overview:
Rationale should explain "why" the opportunity exists. It also defines aspects and implications of the opportunity. This "theme" should be carried out throughout the proposal.
Goals of Analysis:
1. Examine underlying dynamics of the situation
2. Postulate causal relationships
3. Reveal patterns, connections, and meanings that will cause planning to result in action (action plan)

Technical Aspects of Analyzing the Change Opportunity:
1. Etiology: when events/factors tend to be found together or follow each other (cause and contributors)
2. Theory: set of concepts, laws, suppositions that describe and explain phenomena
   a. *Enable user to understand the underlying dynamics and make predictions*
3. Research: a step-by-step progression to build expertise

Quintessence: Analysis and Demonstration of Need
   Variables Affecting Need for Planning:
1. Increased emphasis upon working with "special populations"
2. Accountability
3. Dwindling funds
4. Increased efforts towards external funding
5. Increased competition for available funds
6. Increasing use of technology

Planning concepts:
1. Typically, more responsive to change and action-oriented than traditional research
2. More "optimistic" and developmentally-oriented in its terminology, i.e. use of "opportunity", rather than "problem"; "change agent", rather than "researcher"; "change effort", rather than "problem resolution"

3. Types of change efforts: project, program, policy, and combination
    a. *Project-* short term (6 months or less) resembling program change; often used as a "pilot"
    b. *Program-* provides actual services to consumers during a time span of 6 months or more Examples: providing a workshop series, providing counseling sessions, etc.
    c. *Policy-* changing existing organizational policy, i.e. changing organization through adding a position, changing personnel policy, changing curricula, etc.
    d. *Combination* – a combination effort, usually project/program, where one effort begins and another is "built in" to take its place later on, i.e. a stress management workshop is provided for a month; if all goes well, it will evolve into a regular part of service provision. This would be an example of a project that turns into a program effort
4. When an "opportunity" is implemented, it becomes an "effort"
5. The strongest planning rationale includes both a localized needs assessment AND a review of the related literature: this review can include "fugitive literature", i.e. not periodical literature, but valuable in its own right-examples: annual reports, newsletters, public demographic, personal communications and on-line internet publications

Effective Planning

A *Planned Change Effort* presumes that effective "up front" planning has occurred. The *Change Episode* (cycle) usually depends on the period for which you are funded; however, that does not mean that effective planning ahead of time is unnecessary.

Elements of Effective Planning:
1. Utilization of a *planning team* and/or *advisory board*
    a. Reasons for Using:
        i. can assist in planning from start to finish
        ii. can be especially helpful in accessing populations for
        iii. needs assessments
        iv. can help minimize future conflict/manage obstacles
        v. can generate creative ideas
        vi. can assist with *force-field analyses*
        vii. can be effective source of volunteers
    b. Composition of:
        i. should include *potential restraining forces* (people who might try to hinder your success)
        ii. should include *potential facilitating forces* (people who are not directly responsible for your success but could have a negative impact, if not included)
        iii. should include *potential driving forces* (people who are in positions of power who can ensure success)
        iv. should include members of target population
        v. should include others, as appropriate
        vi. should not be unwieldy in size-consider no more than 10-12
        vii. should include constituencies mandated for grant funds
2. Conducting planning analyses
    a. Force-field analyses (before team composed and after-with team input)
    b. Organizational structure
        i. leadership style: democratic, laissez-faire, authoritarian, situational
        ii. task and maintenance orientations
        iii. agency's missions/effort goals and objectives
    c. Antecedent conditions (includes all of above)
        i. residue from past change efforts: failures and successes
        ii. organizational effort(s) toward planning, to date
3. Demonstrating need
    a. Need = a gap between what you have and what you want
        i. equality – a lack of something that leads to discomfort, contrasted to a problem
        ii. discrimination – a presumption of something that leads to discomfort
4. Considerations in demonstrating need:
    a. Review of mission periodically needed
    b. Mission relates to reality and the future
    c. Working smarter is better than working harder

       d.   Change is based on the realities of the future, not just present factors

       e.   Efforts are made to create the future that's needed-not just the one that is

5.   Types of need:

       a.   Relative need – review of the literature including similar initiatives with comparisons of similar opportunities or programs, as well as expert opinion

       b.   Expressed need – input from the target population:

       c.   Perceived need – survey/interview of the providers of the target population (agency or organization or group) rationale

[These tools are used for assessment when conducted up front and used for evaluation when conducted during the implementation or at the end of the project; the evaluation can become the assessment for a new opportunity or initiative]

6.   Elements of Strategic (focused/targeted) Planning

       a.   Analyses of SWOT's

           i.   Strengths (S)

          ii.   Weaknesses (W)

         iii.   Opportunities (0)

         iv.   Threats (T)

       b.   Tasks of a SWOT

           i.   scoping:

               1.   Who are our consumers?

               2.   Who benefits from change?

         ii.data collecting:

               1.   What are our goals?

               2.   Do we have objectives toward meeting those goals that are result-oriented and measurable?

               3.   What are the needs?

         iii.planning:

               1.   Does our organization (structure, leadership, etc.) match with our mission/goals/objectives?

               2.   What should we do about mismatches; can we reconcile differences, or do we need do some "housekeeping" or "moves"?

               3.   Are we future-oriented?

               4.   What are the **SWOT**'s?

       c.   Implementing and Evaluating

Common Errors in Planning:	
1.	Not thinking "big" enough
2.	Objectives were not result-oriented
3.	Input was not solicited and/or used from key forces
4.	Change agent assumed he/she had the solution beforehand (like researcher bias)
5.	Change agent and/or team set objectives solely on personal perceptions
6.	Assumption that helping professions' planning occurs best at the intuitive level
7.	Change agent/and or team did not think through all the components in planning before beginning

Organizational Structure

In analyzing the change opportunity, consideration should always be given to the organizational structure. Organizations are built around issues. Management of issues depends upon a variety of factors, including: *mission, leadership, and type of organization.*

Definitions:

Mission refers to the overall purpose of the organization.

Leadership refers (very generally) to the preferred approaches, energies, styles modeled within the agency.

Type of Organization refers, in large part, to the responsiveness of the organization to change. Review the organizational chart for "clues" regarding the type of organization and how responsive it may be to change. Terms used to describe the type of organization include: *mechanistic* and *organic*.

Mechanistic organizations are good under stable conditions and resemble what most of us view as "typical" hierarchical, bureaucratic systems. In this type of structure, roles, tasks, communication lines, etc. are all concrete, clear, and rigid. Interaction between members is vertical, and loyalty and obedience to superiors is demanded.

Organic organizations are good under changing conditions. This type of structure involves assignments of roles based upon specialized knowledge. Expertise throughout the system is utilized for attainment of a common (shared) mission; and communication resembles consultation, rather than command. It is theoretically possible for a large organization to demonstrate both types of structure, depending upon the unit; however, overall tone for structure usually filters from the "top-down".

Other factors to consider in regard to organizational structure include: location, population served by the organization, and related demographic/idiosyncratic variables. These factors should be referenced in some manner within the organization's mission statement.

Description of the Organizational Structure within a Planning Document (Proposal)

Description of the Organizational Structure within a planning document will typically be referenced completely or briefly within the Introduction. A more in-depth description is most often included within the Rationale, particularly in regard to the narrative about local need. The description will name or describe without the name (as in a research article where anonymity has been assured) the organization. Included will be information regarding mission, size, leadership, related demographics, and where, within the structure, the proposed will be housed. Sometimes change agents include a copy of the organizational chart as it relates to the proposed. This chart may be included with the text or referenced within the appendices.

The description will specifically describe any organizational variation(s) that may occur as a result of implementation. *If your organizational structure will not be conducive to the opportunity you wish to address, you may want to consider implementation elsewhere. Analysis of the organizational structure plays a significant role in your review of those antecedent conditions.*

EXAMPLE:

STRUCTURE OF ORGANIZATION

ORGANIZATIONAL FLOW CHART

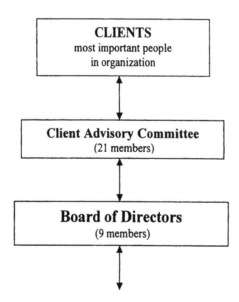

5 Stages of Change:
1. Pre-contemplation
2. Contemplation
3. Preparation
4. Action
5. Maintenance

Change Model Steps
1. Identify the opportunity
2. Analyze the opportunity (gather information for Rationale)
3. Set goals and objectives
4. Design and structure the effort
5. Develop resource plan
6. Implement Effort
7. Monitor the change effort (formative evaluation)
8. Evaluate the final result(s) (summative evaluation)
9. Reassess and stabilize the situation (re-decide)

Analyzing the Change Opportunity
The Rationale should explain "why" the opportunity exists. It also defines aspects and implications of the opportunity. This "theme" should be carried out throughout the proposal.

Goals of Analysis:
1. Examine underlying dynamics of the situation
2. Postulate causal relationships
3. Reveal patterns, connections, and meanings that will cause planning to result in action (action plan)
    a. Analyzing the responses to closed questions, should include a summary of;
        i. the number of individuals who responded to each question
        ii. the proportion of individuals who provided each response
        iii. the frequency of responses for each possibility
        iv. the mean or average score for each question
        v. an indication of the type of distribution – tight or spread, balance or skew
        vi. cross tabulations for different sub-groups within a sample, by gender, ability, or experience
    b. Analyzing the responses to open-ended questions, should include a summary of:
        i. work with individual comments, in a physical, electronic, or scissors cut-and-paste activity
        ii. provisionally, group the comment by topic to which they refer
        iii. on a second pass, and having attempted to use the first set of headings, be prepared to revise and refine to get appropriate precision and suitable coverage
        iv. summarize where that is meaningful, but otherwise list comments verbatim

Needs assessments assist in looking for patterns and interrelationships among data collected.

Technical Aspects of Analyzing the Change Opportunity
1. Etiology: when events/factors tend to be found together or follow each other (causes and contributors)
    a. May exist in social structure, i.e. unemployment resulting from technical change
    b. May exist within individual personality, i.e. person unemployed because he/she can't get along with others
    c. May exist within inadequate human service provision, i.e. lack of training programs
    d. May exist because of transitory social phenomena, i.e. recession causing temporary unemployment
        i. Warning: change agent's perception may bias
2. Theory: set of concepts, laws, and suppositions that describes and explains phenomena
    a. Enable user to understand the underlying dynamics and make predictions
    b. Initially, a broad range of etiologies and theories should be considered: then narrowed-down
3. Research: a step-by-step progression to build expertise
    a. Identify the research area of interest that is broad enough
    b. Develop researchable questions that address several aspects of the broad topic
    c. Conduct a literature review or engage in other research activities such as interviewing, surveys, etc.
    d. Conduct a pilot study that will provide you with preliminary data from which you may develop a larger study

TO DO!

Conduct a **SWOT** analysis.

Sample health and human service professional SWOT topics:
- Conducting *Family Preservation Groups* as a part of unemployment services
- Providing *Activity Grants* for children in the child welfare system, for participation in sports and the arts
- *Parenting Classes* incorporated into the Junior High School curriculum.
- Providing free *Childcare* for parents participating in Drug and Alcohol support meetings
- Providing *Fuel Vouchers* for a three month period of employment when an individual exits the welfare role or unemployment status.

(Add three of your own sample topics)

_____
_____
_____
_____
_____
_____
_____

Identified SWOT Topic: _____

"S" Strengths	"O" Opportunities
"W" Weaknesses	"T" Threats

List at least four examples of fugitive literature.

_____

_____

_____

_____

Key terms and Concepts: Can you define and explain each of the following key terms? Are you prepared to offer brief examples or applicable context for each concept?

Advisory Board:

_____

_____

Analysis:

_____

_____

Authoritarian Style of Leadership:

_____

_____

Change Episode:

_____

_____

Change Model:

_____

_____

Democratic Style of Leadership:

_____

_____

Demonstration of Need:

_____

_____

Driving Forces:

_____

_____

Etiology:

_____

_____

Expressed Need:

_____

_____

Facilitating Forces:

_____

_____

Force Field Analysis:

_____

_____

Fugitive Literature:

_____

_____

Laissez-faire Style of Leadership:

_____

_____

Mechanistic Organization:

_____

_____

Organic Organization:

_____

_____

Organizational Structure:

_____

_____

Perceived Need:

_____

_____

Planned Change Effort:

_____

_____

Planning Team:

_____

_____

Relative Need:

_____

_____

Restraining Forces:

_____

_____

Situational Style of Leadership:

_____

_____

Supposition:

_____
_____

SWOT:

_____
_____

Theory:

_____
_____

Questions:

What did you learn about the process of completing a SWOT analysis?
Explain the significance of each of these **types** of *Planning Team* or *Advisory Board* members:
Potential restraining forces:
Potential facilitating forces:
Potential driving forces:
Members of target population:
Constituencies mandated for grant funds:
Others:
Describe and ideal size for group & why:

Chronicle and Rumination:

This is the space provided to *chronicle* your thoughts and to *ruminate* over the material presented in this chapter along with the references, outside readings, classroom activities, and experiences. Documenting your thoughts and feelings will provide a written account of your *Effective Planning Strategies and Proposal Writing* education.

Chapter Three
Evaluation, Reassessment, and Stabilization

Chapter Outcomes: At the completion of this chapter, activities and assignments, the student will:
1. Understand how to evaluate a change effort.
   a. Understand the importance of formative and summative evaluation
   b. Identify considerations in evaluation: acceptance, cost, system compatibility, confidentiality, staff training, use of information
   c. Identify components of evaluation: inputs, throughputs, outputs, outcomes
   d. Identify how to analyze data
   e. Understand differences/similarities between evaluation and research
2. Define the roles of the Change Agent

Overview:
In order to assess and improve the effectiveness and quality of a change effort, the change agent must address evaluation at all stages of the initiative. Effectual evaluation must consider inputs, throughputs, outputs, and outcomes, in the areas of effort, activities, performance, cost efficiency, and the implementation process. The data necessary for these types of evaluation include client perceptions, third party perceptions, change agent perceptions, concrete measurable information, and client satisfaction. Data analysis techniques include verbatim reporting, summary of data, as well as the implementation of statistical analysis. The evaluation section includes subheadings for *Cost Efficiency, Formative Evaluation* and *Summative Evaluation,* as well as accompanying discussion of evaluative components such as instrumentation, samples, dissemination plan, and criteria for determining "success". Reassessment and Stabilization bring the change episode to closure. The Reassessment provides a specific evaluative function related to the "success" of the change episode, while Stabilization targets refinement of the process and continuation.

Quintessence: Evaluation
   Components to Consider in Evaluation
   1. Inputs: needs, demands, constraints, resources, (including time)
   2. Throughputs: assignment of resources, service delivery, etc. (how effectively are things progressing?)
   3. Outputs: serviced populations—how are they doing at the close of the effort?
   4. Outcomes: results over time, usually obtained through follow-up

   Other considerations related to Need
   1. The complexity of the need (usually more than one contributing factor)
   2. Urgency of the need
   3. Duration of need – how long has the need existed; often correlated to the difficulty of effecting change
   4. What is the scope of control (is this change effort within the power of the change agent or group? If not; probably should not attempt)

   Areas for Evaluation
   1. Effort or activities
   2. Performance or outcomes, i.e. "quality of life" changes
   3. Adequacy of performance
   4. Efficiency (cost)

    5.   Implementation (action plan) process

Data that Can Be Gathered for Evaluation
1. Client perceptions
2. Third party (external evaluator) perceptions
3. Change agent perceptions
4. Hard, measurable information
5. Client satisfaction

Four Scales of Data (the type of data scale determines the type of analysis)
1. *Nominal Scale* is the most elementary of the measurement scales and involves classification by naming based on characteristics. The intent of the nominal scale is to name an object (i.e. 1= Democrat, 2= Republican, 3= Libertarians, 4= No Party). With a nominal scale you can only get a count or a percentage of individuals who fall into a specific category. [can determine Mode]
2. *Ordinal Scale* provides a measure of magnitude. It is possible to tell which scores are smaller or larger than other scores with an instrument that has an ordinal scale. An ordinal scale allows one to rank or order individuals or objects, but that is the extent of the precision. (ranking order i.e. highest to lowest, tallest to shortest, etc.). [can determine Mode and Median]
3. *Interval Scales* have units that are in equal intervals (a difference of five points between 45 and 50 represents the same amount of change as five points between 85 and 90) – a specific measure between i.e. IQ, temperature, etc. [can determine Mode, Median, and Mean]
4. *Ratio Scales* has all the properties of an interval scale and requires the existence of a meaningful zero (i.e. height-because inches are equal units and there is a meaningful zero). [can determine Mode, Median, and Mean]

Data Analysis
1. Data gathering
    a.   Desegregation – separate, more closely pinpointed
    b.   Aggregation – data clustered/gathered together in composite form
2. Authoritative evidence – quoting a recognized authority (individual, group, agency, or organization)

Data Analysis Techniques
1. Selection of the sample group
    a.   Simple Random Selection – every individual in the population has an equal chance of being selected
    b.   Stratified Sample – individuals are selected for the norming group based on certain demographic characteristics (race, gender, socioeconomic level, amount of education, or religion)
    c.   Cluster Sample – involve not selecting individuals, but rather using existing units. Not selecting all students but selecting specific schools from the total list.
2. Descriptive statistics – are used to describe a group of individuals that have been observed
    a.   Measures of Central Tendency
        i.   Mean
        ii. Median
        iii. Mode
    b.   Measures of Dispersion or Validity:
        i.   Range – the distance between the highest and lowest score
        ii. Standard Deviation – the root mean square of the deviations from the mean
3. Centile or centile points – provides the point on a scale below which a certain percentage of cases fall
4. Standard scores – a converted score based on a mean of zero and a standard deviation of one
5. Normal distribution curve – the distribution of scores fall within the theoretical bell shaped curve
6. Correlations – show the degree of relationship between two sets of measures
7. Inferential statistics – (sampling statistics) are used to make inferences about the total population in terms of observed samples of the total population
    a.   Chi Square – a statistical test used to determine the significance of the difference between two sets of data expressed in frequency or categories
    b.   Comparing Means and Proportions – to discover if two groups differ on some ability or trait
8. Data comparisons
    a.   Cross-sectional analysis – looks at all data at the same point in time
    b.   Time comparisons – compares data at two points in time (last year to this year)
    c.   Comparison of 2 or more examples – i.e. one agency to another or rural to urban

In analyzing responses to closed questions, results should be summarized and minimally include:
- the number of students who responded to each question;
- the proportion of students in the class who provided each response;
- the frequency of responses for each possibility;
- the mean or average score for each question;
- an indication of the type of distribution (tight or spread, balanced or skew);
- cross-tabulations for different sub-groups within the sample, by gender, ability, experience, etc.

EXAMPLE:

PARKING SURVEY QUESTIONNAIRE RAW DATA

	1	2	3	4	5
1) How often do you participate in events/activities at the Community Center?	less than once a month	one to three times a month	about once a week	two to three times a week	four or more times a week
	16	12	38	28	12
2) How do you get to the Community Center for activities or functions?	drive or come by car	public transportation	walk	other	
	93	4	8	1	
3) Are you or your spouse or a family member eligible for a persons with disabilities placard?	yes	no	unsure		
	20	82	4		
4) Do you have a person with disabilities-parking placard?	yes	no			
	18	88			
5) How often do you have problems finding parking at the Community Center?	never	seldom	sometimes	often	always
	13	8	38	37	10
6) How often do you have problems finding *persons with disabilities* parking at the Community Center?	never	seldom	sometimes	often	always
	20	2	12	5	2
7) How often do you find cars without persons with disabilities placards in the *persons with disabilities* spots at the Community Center?	never	seldom	sometimes	often	always
	23	48	29	5	1
8) How often are you unable to attend functions at the Community Center because of parking problems?	never	seldom	sometimes	often	always
	46	26	29	4	1
9) Overall, how satisfied are you with the parking at the Community Center?	very dissatisfied	dissatisfied	neutral	satisfied	very satisfied

	18	29	40	16	3
10) Do you think that the parking capacity should be increased at the Community Center?	1 strongly disagree	2 disagree	3 neutral	4 agree	5 strongly agree
	0	1	16	48	41
11) Please list any suggestions you may have to improve the parking at the Community Center.	comments provided	no comments provided			
	25	81			

Similarly, for open-ended questions, you should:

- work with individual comments, in a physical, electronic, or cut-and-paste format
- provisionally group the comments by the topic to which they refer
- on a second pass, and having attempted to use the first set of headings, be prepared to revise and refine to get appropriate precision and suitable coverage
- summarize if certain that responses are common; otherwise list comments verbatim

In computing gain ratio (before and after)

Pre-test	Post-test	Absolute Gain	Gain Ratio
40%	60%	20%	20/60 = .33 (60% away from total)
70%	90%	20%	20/30 = .67 (30% away from total)

EXAMPLE 1:

One hundred and six Parking Survey Questionnaires were voluntarily completed by individuals participating in activities and events at the Crawford Community Center. The results of the assessments demonstrate expressed need by indicating the opinions and concerns of the consumers actively using the Community Center facility and services (See Appendix I). The data indicated that seventy-four percent of the survey participants make use of the Community Center facilities and programs on at least a weekly basis and eighty-eight percent of these individuals drive to the center requiring adequate parking facilities. Eighty-eight percent of the senior consumers reported having problems finding parking at the Community Center, with fifty-seven percent documenting that there were times when they were unable to attend activities or events as a result of the lack of adequate accessible parking. The issue of persons with disabilities parking needs was also addressed in the survey. Of the one hundred and six respondents, 20 individuals indicated that they or a family member were eligible for a persons with disabilities placard, with 4 respondents indicating that they were unsure of their eligibility for the parking placard. Survey question 6 asks these consumers, "How often do you have problems finding persons with disabilities parking at the Community Center?" The responses ranged from 2 individuals selecting the answer seldom, 12 answering sometimes, 5 answering often and 2 individuals answering that they always have problems finding persons with disabilities parking at the Community Center. Also related to the persons with disabilities parking issue, the surveys ask, "How often do you find cars without persons with disabilities placards in the persons with disabilities spots at the community Center?" Seventy-eight percent of the respondents indicated that they have witnessed misuse of the very limited number of persons with disabilities parking spaces at the Community Center. When asked about their overall satisfaction with the parking facilities, thirty-eight percent of the consumers indicated they were neutral and forty-four percent of the respondents indicated being dissatisfied or very dissatisfied with the parking accommodations. The senior consumers were also asked, "Do you think that the parking capacity should be increased at the Community Center?" An overwhelming eighty-four percent indicating that they agree or strongly agree that the parking facilities should be increased. The Parking Survey Questionnaire included an open-ended question to solicit the respondents' comments, con-

cerns, and suggestions regarding the Community Center parking accommodations. Additional comments were provided by 25 of the seniors surveyed. Summary Sampling of comments and concern:
- o People are parking in the fire lane to attend center functions
- o If I am angry about parking, I leave
- o Where do the employees and volunteers park
- o I have to use overflow parking lots two blocks away
- o Some spaces are too far away for even the non-persons with disabilities patrons to access
- o Extra parking lots can be a distance problem
- o Don't book more than one event at the same time
- o We need a better understanding of where parking is located
- o Available parking areas are very hard to walk from
- o Need more parking spaces for special events

Summary Sampling of suggestions:
- o Provide a closer parking areas
- o You need a larger parking facility
- o Build more parking spaces
- o Buy the empty lot across the street for parking
- o Provide a person to transport people from the parking areas away from the center
- o Increase persons with disabilities parking areas
- o Increase the parking around the senior center that do not have meters
- o People not using the center should not park in the center parking lots
- o Parking entrance and exits should be clearly marked so they are not blocked
- o Purchase run down homes nearby and create parking lots

EXAMPLE 2:

Structured interviews were conducted with five Crawford County Community Center consumers. On a voluntary based, these individuals participated in an interview with this change agent. The interview questions were designed to solicit information related to the Property Acquisition for Expanded Parking Facilities Change Effort (See Appendix F). The consumers were asked 17 open ended questions related to the activities, services, and events held at the Crawford County Community Center. Specifically, the questions related to the facility, the parking, and the staff, with the stated intent to improve consumer satisfaction. The consumers were informed that the interviews were conducted in cooperation with Active Aging Inc. and with the permission of Mr. XXXX, CEO. Identification of the consumers by name was Optional. The criteria for the selection of the interviewees included: voluntary participation, individuals 60 or older, participation in community center activities or events at least monthly, and two of the five individuals had identified disabilities that would qualify them for a persons with disabilities placard. The qualitative data compiled from the structured interviews indicates that these five seniors participate in wide variety of Community Center activities, events, and service with a noted frequency of between one and three times a week, and that they drive to each function. All of the respondents indicated satisfaction with current services and programs offered. Interview question 5 asked these consumers; "Are there any obstacles that prevent or hinder your participation in Crawford County Community Center activities, events, or services? And if so, please list and describe".
Summary Sampling of responses:
- o Some of the activities are scheduled at the same time and I can't do two thing at once
- o My husband doesn't always want to participate
- o The weather sometimes effects what we do
- o The parking is really bad some days when there is a lot going on
- o I can't always get in from the parking lot cause I have to park too far away or I park in the fire lane, hope I don't get caught

Related specifically to the expanded parking change effort, question 10 asked interviewees to; Please explain your overall rate of satisfaction with the Crawford County Community Center parking?
Summary Sampling of responses:
- o Oh, it is terrible, especially on days when there is a lot going on here
- o It's good if you get here early, but mid morning and on it gets hard to find parking some days

- o   I just always park down the street so that people who really need to park close to the door can,
- o   I just don't like to walk that far in the rain or cold, but the people who need the persons with disabilities parking should get to park close, someday I might need those spaces too
- o   I think you should tear down those old houses around the corner and put in a new parking building so we don't have to go in and out of the weather
- o   We need more parking, or maybe McDonald's should give the Center some of their parking spaces, you know donate to us old folks

Question 13 asked; "Do you have any suggestions for improvement with the Crawford County Community Center Parking?"
Summary Sampling of suggestions:
- o   Like I said, put in a parking building where those old houses are now
- o   I don't know why we can't use the video lot across the street, it just sits empty
- o   Don't you want to put in a parking lot across the street, I like that idea
- o   We need more parking, especially persons with disabilities spaces
- o   I guess if we could have more parking it would be an improvement

Interviewees were asked two questions related to their participation in fundraising activities and for suggestions for the use of the monies raised by fundraising functions. Two of the respondents indicated that they were actively involved in fundraising activities on a regular basis. One respondent indicated that donations were made to the Crawford County Community Center, another respondent indicated a desire to remain anonymous with regard to contributions, and the final respondent stated that payment was made for meals and services.
Summary sampling of suggested use of fundraising monies:
- o   Tear down those old house and use the money to build a parking building, the city should pay you for the improvement of the property
- o   I think that the Advisory Board uses the money the way it should be used
- o   More outreach services for the home-bound seniors

Question 17 asked; "Is there anything else you would like to add that might improve the activities, events, or services that are provided by the Crawford County Community Center?"
Summary Sampling of suggestions:
- o   Buy the land on Park Avenue of more parking
- o   Vans to pick seniors up at their homes and bring them into the Center
- o   Hire more staff , these people who work at the Center work really hard

---

Components of Evaluation Section:
Subheadings
1. Cost efficiency (if apropos)
2. Formative evaluation
3. Summative evaluation
   a.   Outputs—evaluative results collected immediately after the change effort/episode concludes
   b.   Outcomes—evaluative data collected over time, usually through follow-up surveys or interview
Discussion of
1. Instrument format(s) and sample(s) in appendices
2. Statistics used to compile and analyze data
3. Dissemination plan
4. How you will determine "success"
Problems with Evaluation
1. Role conflict
2. Political issues, i.e. competition for resources
3. Design of evaluation tools
4. Validity and reliability

Reassessment and Stabilization (bringing change episode to closure)

Requirements
1. Input from participants
2. Reflection on meaning
3. Timing
4. Momentum
5. Readiness
6. Acceptance and approval
7. Closure

Reassessment: serves specific evaluative function-to determine overall success for planning "next" episode (to have or not to have)
1. How responsive are/were we to change?
2. Did we fulfill our objectives?
3. Were our design and structure appropriate?
4. Do we have adequate resources to continue?
5. Were the consequences of implementation positive or negative?
6. What did our monitoring (formative evaluation) activities indicate? Could we handle this?
7. Was evaluation adequate?

Stabilization: targets refinement of process
1. How do/Can we integrate with other systems?
2. How do/Can we routinize procedures?
3. How do/Can we develop ongoing support?
4. What happens to the change agent?

Roles of the Change Agent:
1. Critic/reviewer
2. Facilitator/enabler
3. Advocate
4. Interpreter
5. "Closer"

Stabilization
Organizations are built around issues
1. What are the issues, now?
2. Have they changed or remained the same?
3. Does the opportunity still exist or need modification?
4. How do the people, team, providers, target population, feel now?
5. Can your effort be adjusted to address new needs, i.e. resource-wise, time-wise, etc.?
6. Are you, as change agent, still the right person for the role(s) you've played- or should that change?
7. Has enthusiasm remained high or waned?
8. Is there a sense of floundering?
9. Is there momentum to continue?

Common Pitfalls
1. Inflexibility
2. Intolerance for confusion
3. Poor group process
4. Inadequate communication
5. Lack of distributed leadership/ developing leadership among members
6. Lack of follow-through on tasks
7. Turning fears into anger
8. Poor development efforts

Evaluation plan
1. Formative – evaluation during the change effort; monitoring

2. Summative evaluation – evaluation conducted at the end of the change effort
3. Outputs: summative evaluation that occurs immediately after the change effort ends
4. Outcomes: summative evaluation that occurs after a period of time has elapsed—generally, 6 months or more
5. Cost efficiency formulas – demonstrate cost efficiency

EXAMPLES:
As example, if a change agent is working with an initiative to place at-risk clients in job placements, an efficiency formula might be used to evaluate the effectiveness of the effort. In the first efficiency formula, the total cost of the effort is divided by a number of services that have been provided. In this case, the number of services has been determined by totaling interviews conducted by staff with the target population as follows:

Efficiency Formulas:

 # 1: total cost of effort/number of services

$$\frac{\text{Total cost of effort}}{\text{number of services}} = \frac{\$100,000}{4000 \text{ interviews}}$$

$100,000/4000 = $25/unit of service

Depending upon the change effort, $25/unit of service is very cost-efficient. Sometimes, the funding source will provide the formula they wish to be used to determine efficiency and/or the cost per unit of service.

Using the same example of job placement with at-risk clients, cost efficiency could be determined by dividing the cost per unit of service (interview) by an outcome factor. In this hypothetical, let's presume that the expected job placement of clients (outcome factor) will be 20% (.20). Cost efficiency would then be calculated as follows:

 # 2: unit cost/outcome factor

Unit cost=$25
Placement rate (outcome factor) = 20% (.20)
$25/.2=$125/unit output cost

Depending upon the change effort, $125/unit output cost might not be considered cost efficient. On the other hand, $125/unit output cost might be considered cost efficient when services are generally expensive. An example might be when the effort involves medical costs.

EXAMPLE:

1. Evaluation

Change Effort Summary of LEAP Proposal

Bethesda Children's Home is proposing a program design opportunity for a Foster Care Child Activity Scholarship. This program opportunity would facilitate Crawford County foster care children's participation in strengths based Arts, athletics, and structured recreational/educational activities. This proposed L.E.A.P Scholarship Program (Let Everyone Actively Participate) would provide the needed financial resources for Crawford County foster care children to engage in extra-curricular community and school related activities. Through the scholarship, funds would be available for activity participation fees, equipment rental or purchase, the cost of lessons, uniforms expenses, and miscellaneous related expenses.
Bethesda Children's Home is requesting $20,000.00 in HSDF (Human Services Development Funds), as part of the total start up budget of $30,000.00 for the L.E.A.P Scholarship Program (Let Everyone Actively Participate). These HSDF monies along with matching funds from the Bethesda Foundation will be utilized for foster-children's participation in strengths based Arts, athletics, and structured recreational/educational activities.

---

a. Formative Evaluation
Evaluation will be conducted throughout the program implementation. The planning team will meet monthly, during the initial year, in a focus group format to address the issues, obstacles, and program progress. The planning team will also make the determination for the awarding of the LEAP scholarships. Quarterly financial reports will be submitted to the Bethesda Board of Directors as a part of the formative evaluation process.

b.   Summative Evaluation

Evaluation will be completed annually. An evaluation assessment will be presented to all Crawford County foster care children and foster care parents. The Children's Activity Questionnaire and Children's Activities-Foster Parent Questionnaire will be made available for voluntary completion from July 1, 2005 to July 15, 2005. Data from these assessment instruments will be compared with the initial need assessment raw data collected in April of 2004. The results and an analysis will be sent to the funding source and to the Bethesda Board of Directors.

c.   Criteria for Success

Success will be measured by the responses the Crawford County foster children/adolescents and parents provide on the Evaluation Survey Questionnaire. Projected summary samplings from these assessment instruments would include an increase in participation in activities by the foster children/adolescents. This planning team is looking for a 75% participation level in community and school related activities. If less than a 75% participation level is indicated from the assessment tool, this planning team will consider the project unsuccessful.

EXAMPLE:

Change Effort Summary of Crawford County Senior Community Center Property Acquisition For Expanded Parking Facilities Proposal

The Crawford County Community Center, a non-profit organization, provided 43,830 center service visits and served 2303 area seniors last year. Additionally, the facility served 27,952 meals to 1275 Crawford County seniors (Annual report, 2008). On an average day the center may sponsor 8 to 15 separate activities/events as well as schedule rental groups for fundraising to support the community services. The Community Center parking capacity is 81 parking spaces; to accommodate a Senior Center usage averaging between 200 and 300 consumers a day, parking for 35 staff, volunteer parking, and parking for 7 agency vehicles (XXXX, CEO personal communication, June 12, 2008). Active Aging Inc. is requesting $275,000.00 in grant funds, as part of the total budget of $377,000.00, for the acquisition and renovations of property to create 30 additional parking spaces and the conversion of existing parking to create 12 persons with disabilities parking spaces.

Formative Evaluation

Evaluation will be conducted throughout the change effort. The Planning team will meet monthly during the change effort implementation period. The members will meet in a focus group format, addressing issues, obstacles, and change effort progress.

Summative Evaluation

An evaluation assessment will be presented to a minimum of 200 individuals participating in activities or events at the Crawford County Community Center to assess the change effort completion. A Parking Survey Questionnaire will be made available for voluntary completion between January 1, 2009 and January 15, 2009 (See Appendix E). The Parking Survey Questionnaire consists of 10 questions. There are two forced answer questions related to persons with disabilities eligibility that require a yes/no response. A Likert scale is used to respond to 8 questions related to personal Crawford County Community Center usage and parking. An open ended question is also included in the survey, soliciting suggestions for improvement of the parking conditions at the Crawford County Community Center. In addition, the change agent will also assess change effort success through the completion of five structure interviews with senior citizens (See Appendix F). The criteria for the selection of the interviewees will include: voluntary participation, individuals 60 or older, participation in community center activities or events at least monthly, and two of the five individuals will have identified disabilities that would qualify them for a persons with disabilities placard. Data from these assessment instruments will be compared with the initial need assessment raw data collected in June of 2008. The results will be sent to the funding source and the Active Aging, Inc. Governing Board and Advisory Board. Evaluation will be conducted at the end of the change effort.

Appendix E
Change Effort Summary of Property Acquisition For Expanded Parking Facilities Proposal
Parking Survey Questionnaire

Please complete the following questions by circling the correct answer.

1) How often do you participate in events/activities at the Community Center?

1	2	3	4	5
less than once a month	one to three times a month	about once a week times a week	two to three times a week	four or more

2) How do you get to the Community Center for activities or functions?

1	2	3	4
drive or	use public	walk	other _____
come by car	transportation		

3) Are you or your spouse or a family member eligible for a persons with disabilities placard?

1	2	3
yes	no	unsure

4) Do you have a persons with disabilities parking placard?

1	2
yes	no

5) How often do you have problems finding parking at the Community Center?

1	2	3	4	5
never	seldom	sometimes	often	always

6) How often do you have problems finding **persons with disabilities** parking at the Community Center?

1	2	3	4	5	6
never	seldom	sometimes	often	always	N/A

7) How often do you find cars without persons with disabilities placards in the **persons with disabilities** spots at the Community Center?

1	2	3	4	5
never	seldom	sometimes	often	always

8) How often are you unable to attend functions at the Community Center because of parking problems?

1	2	3	4	5
never	seldom	sometimes	often	always

9) Overall, how satisfied are you with the parking at the Community Center?

1	2	3	4	5
very dissatisfied	dissatisfied	neutral	satisfied	very satisfied

10) Do you think that the parking capacity should be increased at the Community Center?

1	2	3	4	5
strongly disagree	disagree	neutral	agree	strongly agree

11) Please list any suggestions you may have to improve the parking at the Community

_____
_____
_____
_____
_____
_____
_____
_____
_____

Appendix F
Change Effort Summary of Property Acquisition For Expanded Parking Facilities Proposal

Structured Interview Questions
Preliminary Information:
      Introduction of Change Agent, Larry Dickson

Statement of Purpose of interview: To talk with senior citizens to obtain information about the activities, services, and events held at the Crawford County Community Center, related to the facility, parking, and staff, in order to improve consumer satisfaction. These interviews are being conducted in cooperation with Active Aging Inc. and with the permission XXXXX, CEO.

Consumer's Name: _____
   (optional)
Senior Citizen: yes / no
Are you eligible for persons with disabilities parking? yes / no

1. What activities, events, and/or services do you currently participate in through the Crawford County Community Center?
2. How often do you attend/participate in activities, events, or services at the Crawford County Community Center?
3. Are there other programs or services you would be interested in participating in at the Crawford County Community Center? If so what services or programs and when?
4. How satisfied are you with the activities, events, and services offered at the Crawford County Community Center?
5. Are there any obstacles that prevent or hinder your participation in Crawford County Community Center activities, events, or services? Please list and describe.
6. How do you get to and from the Crawford County Community Center?
7. Do you have any problems or concerns with this means of transportation? Explain.
8. Would you be interested in assistance with transportation to and from the Crawford County Community Center? What types of assistance would you be interested in participating in?
9. Please explain your overall rate of satisfaction with the Crawford County Community Center facility?
10. Please explain your overall rate of satisfaction with the Crawford County Community Center parking?
11. Please explain your overall rate of satisfaction with the Crawford County Community Center staff?
12. Do you have any suggestions for improvement with the Crawford County Community Center facility?
13. Do you have any suggestions for improvement with the Crawford County Community Center parking?
14. Do you have any suggestions for improvement with the Crawford County Community Center staff?
15. Do you participate or volunteer in any of the Active Aging Foundation fundraising activities? Explain.
16. How would you want to direct the monies raised through the Active Aging Foundation fundraising activities? Explain.
17. Is there anything else you would like to add that might improve the activities, events, or services that are provided by the Crawford County Community Center?

Thank you for your cooperation and time.

Criteria for Success

Success will be measured by the responses senior center consumers provide on the Evaluation Survey Questionnaires and information gathered during the five structured interviews. Projected summary samplings from these assessment instruments would include an increase in satisfaction rating with the overall parking facilities, an increased availability of convenient accessible persons with disabilities parking accommodations, and an increase of Crawford County Community Center services and activities by the senior citizens of Meadville and the surrounding areas. This change agent is looking for a 75% satisfaction rating with the parking facilities and persons with disabilities parking availability as a result of the completed change effort. If less than a 75% increase in satisfaction is indicated from the assessment tools, this change agent will consider the change effort unsuccessful.

Other sources for information about data analyses include George (1999), Glanz (2006), and Stringer and Dwyer (2005). If complex statistical analyses are being considered, Glanz provides a good overview.

For most audiences, however, it is advisable to keep data simple—clear, concise, and readily understood.

TO DO!
Activities:
#1
Identify the following for your Change Effort:

Inputs:
_____
_____

Throughputs:
_____
_____

Outputs:
_____
_____

Outcomes:
_____
_____

#2 Develop the Cost Efficiency Formula for your Change Effort, and explain:

_____ = _____ = _____

Explain:
_____
_____

Key terms and Concepts: Can you define and explain each of the following key terms? Are you prepared to offer brief examples or applicable context for each concept?

Cost Efficiency:
_____
_____

Dissemination Plan:
_____
_____

Efficiency Formula:
_____
_____

Formative Evaluation:
_____
_____

Implementation Plan:
_____
_____

Inputs:
_____
_____

Outcomes:
_____
_____

Outputs:
_____
_____

Reassessment:

_____
_____

Reliability:

_____
_____

Stabilization:

_____
_____

Summative Evaluation:

_____
_____

Throughputs:

_____
_____

Validity:

_____
_____

Acceptance:

_____
_____

Confidentiality:

_____
_____

Questions:

Describe each of the following roles of the Change Agent:
Critic/Reviewer:
Facilitator:
Advocate:
Interpreter:
Closer:

Chronicle and Rumination:

This is the space provided to *chronicle* your thoughts and to *ruminate* over the material presented in this chapter along with the references, outside readings, classroom activities, and experiences.

Chapter 4
Grant Writing

Chapter Outcomes: At the completion of this chapter, activities and assignments, the student will:
1. Develop a Change Effort proposal
2. Identify and explain the components of a typical Grant Proposal
3. Outline the key components of a Change Effort
4. Compose a cover letter for a Change Effort
5. Write a summary for a Change Effort
6. Understand the roles of Goals and Objectives within the change process.
   a. Define and develop Goals and Objectives and their relationship to an agency's mission
   b. Distinguish between effective and ineffective Goals and Objectives
   c. Develop an action plan from Goals and Objectives

Overview:
The idea of a perfect proposal is a myth. The key to successful grant writing begins with a proposal that is true to who you are (congruent with the mission statement of the organization), that reflects what you do (congruent with the vision of the organization), and realistically identifies what you will need to complete the Change Effort. Presentation, organization, and clarity are critical issues for RFP (Request for Proposals) review committees. Following the RFP guidelines ensures that the reviewers can find the information, especially when making comparisons with other proposals. A strong proposal can produce substantial income for your non-profit organization; enabling the organization to enhance general operating budgets, fund special projects, increase capacity building opportunities, fund capital improvements and equipment purchases, and generate endowment growth.

Quintessence: Grant Writing

Grant Writing Tips
Steps Prior to Writing Proposal
1. Review various funding sources to determine which source best fits your interest and planned project

Areas of financial need for an organization:
   a. Enhance general operating budgets – to cover the costs associated with running an organization, to meet consumers needs
   b. Fund special projects – specific funds to institute a new project, start a new program, enhance an existing program, or a combination design project
   c. Increase capacity building opportunities – this specific project is designed to increase fundraising or organizational capacity to support program/organizational development
   d. Fund capital improvements and equipment purchases – (also known as Capital Campaigns) produce a specified financial goal specifically designated for: the purchase of land, building construction, renovations, equipment purchases, etc.
   e. Generate endowment growth – the principle endowment funds are invested for the organization and the generated income from the investments are used for operating expenses
2. *CONTACT THE PROGRAM DIRECTOR OR CONTACT PERSON* from the agency or foundation you are interested in submitting the proposal to.
3. Contact the grants office. The grants office will provide direction on all steps necessary for preparation. Direction as to impact institution.

4. Contact colleagues to discuss the planned project. Ask colleagues if they would be willing to review the proposal and provide input prior to submission.

5. If the project will involve other institutions or outside agencies, contact these agencies regarding their support and commitment to the project. Specify their involvement and begin the process of collecting letters of support for the project.

6. If possible, obtain a copy of a funded proposal. Review funded proposal closely for presentation, content and budget.

Proposal Preparation

1. Review the application material closely. Determine what questions, priorities and criteria will have to be addressed in the text.

2. List all items that will have to be addressed during proposal preparation that may require information from additional sources that may require additional time to prepare:
   a. Target population
   b. Geographical area
   c. Matching requirements
   d. Institutional expertise
   e. Partnerships/linkages

3. Follow all criteria and address all priorities in the application. Use bold heading to make it easy for reviewers to locate each section of the project. Follow the guidelines as to how the proposal should be presented and organized.

4. Be sure to address the following items in your proposal.
   a. *Need/Rationale*- Why is the program needed in your community? Provide statistics to support statements concerning need.
   b. *Objectives*- Clearly and succinctly define objectives of the project. If working with outside agencies or other institutions, explain how there will be a coordination of effort versus duplication of effort.
   c. *Evaluation*- Explain how you will determine that the program has met the objectives outlined in your proposal.
   d. *Organization*- Explain why your organization is qualified to implement the program. Explain how the program fits into the mission of your institution. Explain the support the program will receive in personnel, resources, expertise, and experience.
   e. *Continuation of Program* – Explain how you plan to continue the program at the end of the grant-funded period. I.e. other sources of support you will seek; institutional commitment to continue project.
   f. *Budgetary Items*- Explain major budgetary items and why these purchases are necessary for the successful completion of the program

5. Electronic proposal submission – If funders are requesting electronic submission, be sure to review guidelines for submission. Generally, change agents must be issued a code for submission well in advance of the actual submission deadline. Additionally, funders may have limited capacity for receipt of proposals, so change agents need to exercise caution when trying to submit immediately before deadline.

Finally, be aware of any restrictions on resubmission. Frequently, funders will accept only the final submission, so make sure that you submit in final form because retrieval may be impossible!

EXAMPLE #1:

Budget

The following is a list of project costs, listing all items that are necessary for the Property Acquisition for Expanded Parking Facilities Change Effort to take place.

Property Acquisition for Expanded Parking Facilities Change Effort	Grant Funds	Active Aging Foundat matching funds	Total
Purchase of property	$225,000.00		$225,000.00
Lot improvements: [signage, curbing, drainage, and paving]	$ 50,000.00	$100,000.00	$150,000.00

Yearly increased operational costs [taxes, snow removal, greens upkeep & repairs]		$2,000.00	$2,000.00
Total for Budget	$275,000.00	$102,000.00	$377,000.00

EXAMPLE #2:

Social Equity 2007-2008 Grant Program
Project Budget

Expenditure	Requested Grant	University Contribution	Other Revenue Source	Total
Salaries				
Dr. Salene Cowher, Project Director *	1,000	180		1180
Student Wages				
Graduate Student 1 student x $4.75 x 20 hrs. x 45 wks.	4,275	325		4,600
Undergraduate Student 5 students x $4.75 x 71 hrs.	1,686	125		1,811
Operating Expenses				
Postage, Telephone, Duplicating		600		600
Housing / Meals	6,539			6,539
Other				
Stipend for Presenters 20 presenters x $75/person	1,500			1,500
TOTALS	15,000	1,230	0	16,230

* Project Director is on a 9-month contract.
 Compensation is for the preparation and supervision of the summer program.

Itemized Budget

CATEGORY I – Instructional Salaries		LOCAL	FEDERAL	TOTAL
1.1	Mary Kelly, Associate Professor 12 month, 20% effort $23,629.	$4,725	$ 0.	$4,725.
1.2	Salene Cowher, Associate Professor 12 month, 100% effort $23,629.	0.	23,629.	23,629.
1.3	Paraprofessional II, Counselor 12 month, 100% effort $12,550.	0.	12,550.	12,550.
TOTALS		**$4,725.**	**$36,179.**	**$40,904.**

CATEGORY II – Fringe Benefits				
2.1	Mary Kelly 33%	$1,559.	$0.	$1,559.
2.2	Salene Cowher 33%	0.	7,797.	7,797.
2.3	Paraprofessional 33%	0.	4,141.	4,141.
TOTALS		**$1,559.**	**$11,938.**	**$13,497.**

CATEGORY II – Itemized Benefits			
Vision (0.4 %)	$19.	$145.	$164.
Dental (2.0 %)	94.	724.	818.
Blue Cross (8.6 %)	406.	3,110.	3,517.
Major Medical (1.0 %)	47.	362.	409.
Total Disability (0.9 %)	43.	325.	369.
Life Insurance & Dependent Life Insurance (0.6 %)	29.	217.	245.
F.I.C.A. (7.0 %)	331.	2,532.	2,863.
PA Unemployment Compensation (2.0 %)	94.	724.	818.
Workmen's Compensation (2.0 %)	94.	724.	818.
TIAA – CREF (8.5 %)	402.	3,075.	3,477.
TOTALS	**$1,559.**	**$11,938.**	**$13,497.**

CATEGORY III – Other Instructional Costs				
Instructional Materials & Supplies				
3.1	Career Books / Career Library	$0.	$400.	$400.
3.2	Printing / Program Information	0.	1,000.	1,000.
Contracted Services				
3.3	Consultants, Career Specialist Speakers	0.	300.	300.
TOTALS		**$0.**	**$1,700.**	**$1,700.**

Itemized Budget Continued…

TOTALS	LOCAL	FEDERAL	TOTAL
Category I	$4,725.	$36,179.	$40,904.
Category II	$1,559.	$11,938.	$13,497.
Category III	$0.	$1,700.	$1,700.
	$6,284.	**$49,817.**	**$56,101.**

Additional Grant Writing Tips:
1. Present a well thought-out presentation.
2. Use a positive writing style, based on facts and practice, which contains some "emotional attraction" for the funder.

3. The proposal should be visually attractive.
   a. Fonts should be consistent, as specified by the funder/RFP.
   b. Logo (pictograph) is a symbol that quickly identifies the organization (i.e. Nike check mark). Thought should be put into the design to ensure that the design symbolizes what your organization does, what you stand for, what services you provide, and why people should choose your organization.
   c. Change Model can be an attractive method of graphic representation of the entire Change Effort. Each line, shape, letter, and color can be useful in sending a message to funders, consumers, and supporters, conveying the significance of your Change Effort. Avoid trying to incorporate too much symbolism into your Change Model.

EXAMPLE:

Change Model:
Leadership Development
Program Goals

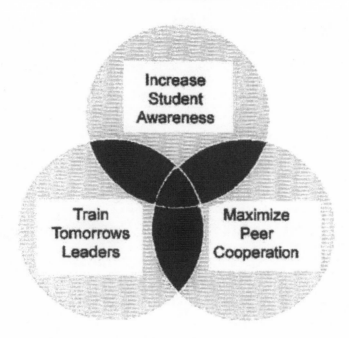

4. Proposals should be printed on quality paper with a print quality suitable to clearly produce the graphics and font style of the proposal.
5. When possible, plan to submit the proposal four to six months before you need the funds.
6. Avoid the use of slang or lingo and don't overwrite.
7. Solicit honest, professional feedback on your proposal from colleagues, writers, and representatives from funding organizations.
8. Don't be afraid to revise and/or edit!

Grant Proposal Format

Always follow the instructions; *call the funding source for clarification.*
Standard Format:
- Cover letter
- Table of contents
- Summary
- Introduction
- Need/Rationale
- Objectives

- Method
- Evaluation
- Resource Plan (includes Budget when external funds are pursued)
- Appendices

1. **Cover Letter**
   a. Type on organization letterhead
   b. Address it to the correct person and office-check the RFP for this info
   c. Check the instruction to see if package is judged to be on time by "Date Received" or by "Date Post-marked"
   d. Briefly describe the proposal – one-half page
   e. How much money needed
   f. How many people helped
   g. Always include the same number of cover letters as proposals
2. **Table of Contents**
   a. Include if proposal is over seven (7) pages:
   b. List Sections plus page numbers by Roman numerals
   c. List appendices plus number by Roman numerals
   d. Number pages from front to back using Arabic numbers including the appendices.
3. **Summary**
   - If document is more than ten (10) pages, include a one-page Summary—like a news release. Hit strengths of the Objectives, Methods, Evaluation and Budget; what will *sell* the project?

TO DO!

Activities:

#1. Identify the following items to be addressed in the proposal preparation:

Target Population:
_____
_____
_____

Geographical Area:
_____
_____

Matching Requirements:
_____
_____
_____

Institutional Expertise:
_____
_____
_____

Partnerships/Linkages:
_____
_____
_____

#2. Outline the following KEY components of your Change Effort:
   A. Need/Rationale:
_____

_____

B. Objectives: _____
_____
_____

C. Evaluation: _____
_____
_____

D. Organization: _____
_____
_____

E. Continuation of Program: _____
_____
_____

F. Budgetary Items: _____
_____
_____

#3. Compose the Cover Letter for your Change Effort.

#4. Write a summary for you Change Effort.

Key terms and Concepts: Can you define and explain each of the following key terms? Are you prepared to offer brief examples or applicable context for each concept?

Direct Costs:
_____

Foundations:
_____

Indirect Costs:
_____

Matching Funds:
_____

Partnerships/Linkages:
_____

Private Sector:
_____

Public Sector:
_____

RFP:
_____
_____

Questions:

List the types of expenditures included in a grant proposal:

List and explain the ten components of a standard Grant Proposal format:

Chronicle and Rumination:

This is the space provided to *chronicle* your thoughts and to *ruminate* over the material presented in this chapter along with the references, outside readings, classroom activities, and experiences. Documenting your thoughts and feelings will provide a written account of your *Effective Planning Strategies and Proposal Writing* education.

Chapter Five
Methods

Chapter Outcomes: At the completion of this chapter, activities and assignments, the student will:

1. Understand how to develop the Methods section of a Change Effort proposal
2. Understand the relevance of Goals and Objectives to Methods
3. Understand the relationship between Methods and Resource Planning
4. Understand the use of Gantt charts

Overview:
The Methods section provides the details of how the Change Agent and/or the organization will carry out the goals and objectives of the Change Effort. Specifically, these are the strategies, activities, or action steps methodically designed to accomplish the Change Effort. This section of the proposal should include the established methods, initiation and ending dates for the action steps, identification of responsible person for the implementation of each action step, and identification of participants. There should be congruence between the Methods Section, the Needs Statement (Rationale), and the Goals and Objectives of the Change Effort. The Methods Section should give the funder(s) an accurate picture of the important action steps designed to accomplish each Goal and each Objective of the Change Effort. The relationship between the Methods and funding request (Budget) should be clear.

Quintessence: Planning concepts

1. Typically, more responsive to change and action-oriented than traditional research
2. More "optimistic" and developmentally oriented, i.e. use of "opportunity", rather than "problem"; "change agent", rather than "researcher"; "change effort". Rather than "problem resolution"
3. When an "opportunity" is implemented, it becomes an "effort"
4. The strongest planning rationale includes both localized needs assessment AND a review of the related literature; this review can include "fugitive literature". i.e. not periodical literature, but valuable in its own right

Methods Chart					
Action Steps	Initiation Date	Individual(s) Responsible	Identified Participants	Required Resources	Completion Date

Methods: includes brief discussion of *Design* (project, program, policy, combination) and *Action Plan* (Activities). Activities will frequently be formatted with the related Objective. *Gantt Charts,* which are used to reflect time frames for completion of Activities, are often included without need for any narrative.

The Methods section frequently highlights only the Action Plan, with narrative sparse and only "as needed". The change agent should make sure that the Methods account for all expenditures that are included within the Resource Plan. In addition, Objectives are often used as the impetus for development of related Activities. When Objectives are clearly measurable, linked to Activities, and assist in accounting for items noted within the Resource Plan, funders are more inclined to approve the Change Effort. Goals and Objectives are frequently identified specifically within a planning document and/or during planning discussions. These may be repeated as a separate listing within Methods or linked to Activities in a Gantt chart format.

Example of goal Statement and Related Objectives:

Goal 1. To enhance the self-esteem of single parents

> *Objective 1A:* to provide testing services to all single parents enrolled in the fall, 2009 Cowher Self-Esteem Improvement Program
>
> *Objective 1B:* to utilize test results in providing individual counseling sessions for all single parents enrolled in the fall, 2009 Cowher Self-Esteem Improvement Program
>
> *Objective 1C:* to conduct post-testing with all single parents enrolled in the fall, 2009 Cowher Self-Esteem Improvement Program that reflects a 50% increase in self-esteem

Discussion: Note breadth of Goal. Also note the elements included with each *Objective 1A:* direction of intended change=to provide testing services: time frame=fall, 2009; target population=single parents enrolled in Cowher Self-Esteem Improvement Program; measurable criterion=all (single parents) *1B:* direction of intended change=to utilize test results in providing individual counseling sessions; time fall=fall, 2009; target population=single parents enrolled in Cowher Self-Esteem Improvement Program; measurable criterion=all (single parents) *1C:* direction of intended change=to conduct post-testing that reflects an increase in self-esteem; time frame=fall, 2009; target population=single parents enrolled in Cowher Self-Esteem Improvement Program; measurable criteria=all (single parents) & 50% increase in self-esteem (according to post-tests). Each Goal should have at least two Objectives. This section is typically no more than 2-3 pages in length.

Example of Objective linked to Related Activities:

Objective 1A: to provide testing services to all single parents enrolled in the fall, 2009 Cowher Self-Esteem Improvement Program

Date	Activity
7/09-8/09	Recruit parents for the program
	Order tests
	Send reminders to enrollees
	Make sure that tests and related materials have arrived
9/3/09	Welcome parents to the program
	Explain tomorrow' testing
	Make sure that testing materials and examiners are ready
9/4/09	Test enrollees
	Score tests

The change agent should review all activities to ensure that nothing has been omitted that is necessary for the Change Effort to take place. The Methods should include all planning components. In addition, the change agent should review the Resource Plan to make sure that all activities can be implemented with the Resources as outlined.

Resource Plan: Should include ALL Resources necessary for change effort to take place. Typical items to include: Personnel, Equipment, Space, Utilities, Materials, and Services. If a *Budget* is needed, the *general format is a zero-based, line-item budget.* Such a budget presumes that no money has been carried over in any fashion from another endeavor, budget, etc. This budget is written item-by-item, with "item" referring to a category of expenses. Typical items include: Personnel, Equipment, Space, Utilities, materials, and Services. The Budget would include only those line items that are not being otherwise provided and only those items that the funding source will provide. Some funding sources, for example, will not fund equipment. Personnel line-items will typically be subdivided into Salaries and Benefits, with an itemized listing of costs for Benefits. Salaries at the level of the Personnel being requested and related Benefits costs are readily obtained through grants offices and personnel offices. ALL proposals include a Resource Plan, even if a Budget is not necessary. Any item in the budget that is atypical for efforts, such as yours, and/or especially costly should be explained in *Budget Notes*. Budget Notes are usually provided in a footnote form at the end of the budget. Items that are described in Budget Notes usually have asterisks (*) placed at the end of their line on the budget, with an accompanying asterisk (*) next to the budget Note. Think of the format for footnotes, and you should understand this concept. Some funding sources will insist that costs be computed in budget Notes or on the Budget line per item. For example, if you were budgeting for Duplicating service costs for $10.00, the funder might want you to note that this reflects 50 copies @ $.20 per copy. They might want this breakdown included on the budget line, itself, or in a Budget Note. The Resource Plan is typically no more than two pages long.

TO DO!

Activities:

#1. Develop a set of Activities to match your Change Effort. Link at least two of these to your Objectives.

_____
_____
_____
_____

#2. How do your Activities and related Objectives assist in the potential attainment of your Goals?

_____
_____
_____
_____

Key terms and Concepts: Can you define and explain each of the following key terms? Are you prepared to offer brief examples or applicable context for each concept?

Action Plan:

_____
_____

Activities:

_____
_____

Gantt Chart:

_____
_____

Methods:

_____
_____

Objectives:

_____
_____

Resource Plan:

_____
_____

Chronicle and Rumination:

> This is the space provided to *CHRONICLE* your thoughts and to *RUMINATE* over the material presented in this chapter along with the references, outside readings, classroom activities, and experiences. Documenting your thoughts and feelings will provide a written account of your *Effective Planning Strategies and Proposal Writing* education.
>
> _____
> _____
> _____
> _____
> _____
> _____
> _____
> _____
> _____
> _____
> _____
> _____
> _____
> _____
> _____
> _____
> _____
> _____
> _____
> _____
> _____
> _____
> _____
> _____
> _____
> _____
> _____
> _____
> _____
> _____
> _____
> _____
> _____

Chapter 6
Ethical and Legal Considerations

Chapter Outcomes: At the completion of this chapter, activities and assignments, the student will:
1. Identify and explain the trends influencing the need to change
2. Identify the declining resources that influence the need for a Change Effort
3. List ethical issues critical to a Change Effort
4. Identify advocacy groups and/or existing advisory boards that may be of assistance to a Change Effort
    a. Explain the importance of advocacy groups and/or existing advisory boards to the Change Effort
    b. Identify contact information for these advocacy groups/advisory boards
5. Identify new technologies that may affect a Change Effort
6. Describe the primary differences between civil liabilities and criminal liabilities
7. Understand the three types of disclosure and provide examples of how these requirements would be met in a Change Effort
8. List and explain the four key points of privileged communication

Overview:
Both ethical and legal guidelines influence professional practice; yet there are differences between the two entities. Laws are related to a body of *rules*, while ethics are a body of *principles* that address proper conduct. Therefore, ethics and laws sometimes focus on different aspects or issues. The focus of both, however, is the protection of people and rights.

Need for Change: There is a tendency in human services to plan for services rather than meeting needs; delivery systems become fixed and inflexible.

Trends influencing need to change:
1. Increasing focus on needs of special populations
2. Decreasing in resources available for human service programs
3. Increasing pressures for accountability in human services
4. Introduction of new techniques for management and direct service personnel

Trend #1
Needs of special populations
    Discrimination:
        A. Perpetuated by addressing symptoms rather than causes. For example; giving money to poor parents when they may need retraining, housing etc.
        B. Recipients excluded from decision-making. Successful change efforts are more likely to occur when participants fell committed to the process from the very beginning.

Trend #2
Declining resources
        A. Few programs are self supporting and have grown increasingly dependent upon external funds.
        B. Open-ended funding has changed into block grants
        C. Decreasing amounts of federal monies that have been budgeted for human service programs
        D. The decline has necessitated ongoing and regular review of service quality and change opportunities

Trend #3
Accountability
- A. Enhanced legal obligation to account for terms of contracted transactions
- B. Obligations to public, agency, and client to maximize effectiveness and efficiency
- C. Ethical obligations involving change opportunities to consumers, funders, research
  - i. Responsibility to accurately report the findings (deliberate misconstruction of assessment or evaluative findings is unethical, but not uncommon in grant writing)
  - ii. Responsibility to caution stakeholders not to generalize findings to situations beyond the scope of the assessment or evaluation
  - iii. Responsibility associated with limits of competency – if the change agent is not qualified to conduct the assessment of evaluations, he/she is obligated to:
    1. gain the appropriate experience, knowledge, and/or certification through education or research
    2. contract or collaborate with an expert who is qualified to conduct the assessment, evaluation, or research
  - iv. Responsibility to respect the rights of the consumer (targeted population)
    1. right to participate by choice
    2. right to informed consent: purpose, risks, and responsibility
    3. right to anonymity – no disclosure of identity
    4. right to confidentiality – no disclosure of their actions or responses
    5. right to withdrawal without negative consequences
    6. right to receive full disclosure
    7. right to evaluation findings

Responsibilities:

Public: public funds and sanctions human services; taxes provide major share of funding

Agency: statements of intent (program goals and objectives, plans, or contracts for purchase of services) become basis for staff accountability to agency

Consumer: (obviously most important) consumer investing time, energy, even money in belief that service/mix of services will improve his/her quality of life

Trend #4
Expanding knowledge and changing technology
- A. Procedures, methodologies, processes must be assessed
- B. Technology must be reviewed based upon professional, ethical and legal guidelines

Note: ***Change is seldom welcomed by all!**

Risks:
1. Loss of colleague/community support (i.e. implementing a new testing program) may occur.
2. Effort may be seen as diverting from major job responsibilities.
3. Direct service personnel may be seen as having limited knowledge about total operation.
4. A worker's reputation may be challenged.
5. May affect one's future and job security.

Possible positive results
1. There are always people interested in helping to build a base for moral, emotional, professional, and financial support.
2. Grievance procedures etc. can protect human services professional
3. Can bring professional credibility status and prestige to those involved.

Potential Legal Issues
Civil case- acting wrongly; failing to act
Criminal case- governmental involvement
Privileged communication:
1. Must originate in confidence
2. Confidentially must be essential to relationship
3. Relationship needs to be fostered

4. Injury from disclosure greater than benefit
   a. Example: Tarasoff vs. Regents University of California (1976): exercising "reasonable care":
      i. danger
      ii. identifiable victim

In Tarasoff v. Regents of the University of California, the parents of a girl who had been murdered by a client at the university hospital sued the University Regents, four psychotherapists, and the campus police. The parents alleged that the defendants were liable for failing to confine the client and warn their daughter.

Group work- no case law; privileged communication does not apply.

Record keeping- business and clinical

1. Documentation should be undertaken in circumstances where a helping professional's actions or inaction may be called into question.
2. Documentation may be needed when:
   a. One is accused of unethical or illegal behavior.
   b. A client is a danger to self or others
   c. A client is involved in a legal controversy
3. Documentation efforts should begin immediately.
4. When documenting for self-protection, as much detail as possible should be included. Dates, times events occurred, and words spoken should be included in as much detail as possible. Only factual information should be included. Personal observations, not based upon fact, should be kept separate or eliminated from documentation files.
5. If a need for documentation arises after the fact, a summary of what happened should be recorded.
6. Documentation files should include originals of any pertinent documents retained by the helping professional.
7. Records kept for documentation should be kept secure. Originals of records should never be released-only copies.

Electronic formats:

1. Security of data becomes an issue and the professional has the ethical and legal obligation of insuring that electronic client data is secured according to Health Insurance Portability and Accountability Act (HIPAA). For help in determining whether or not you/your agency is covered under HIPAA, visit the website for the Centers for Medicare and Medicaid Services at http://www.cms.hhs.gov/
2. Safety of data involves the need to back up electronic records and data so that they can be retrieved in the event of equipment failure or loss. (Back up data files must also comply with the HIPAA regulations for security).

Note: Helping professionals should always be familiar with professional ethical standards in their field. Check state credentialing (licensure, certification) boards and accompanying legislation.

Credentialing Links for Helping Professions

- **Commission on Rehabilitation Counselor Certification (CRCC)** - board-certifies U.S. professional counselors in the specialty of rehab counseling
- **Council for Accreditation of Counseling & Related Educational Programs (CACREP)** - accredits career, geriatric, marriage & family, mental health/community, and school counseling programs, plus doctoral programs in professional counseling research/teaching/clinical supervision (a.k.a. "counselor education"), in the U.S.; has an on-line directory of accredited programs; an affiliate of the American Counseling Assoc.
- **Council on Rehabilitation Education (CORE)** - accredits rehab counseling programs in the U.S.; has an on-line directory of accredited programs
- **National Academy of Certified Family Therapists (NACFT)** - board-certifies U.S. professional counselors in the specialty of marriage & family counseling; an affiliate of the American Counseling Assoc.
- **National Board for Certified Counselors (NBCC)** - board-certifies U.S. professional counselors in the specialties of mental health, school, and substance abuse counseling; has an on-line feature that enables certificants and the general public to check on board certification status, review board policies, pay renewal fees, and submit a contact information update; an affiliate of the American Counseling Assoc.
- **National Association of Social Workers (NASW)** – is the largest association of social workers in the world; offers several types of certifications; maintains professional standards and provides professional development opportunities; includes links to social workers websites
- **National Association of School Psychologists (NASP)** – provides professional standards, training, professional development and resources for professionals, families and educators

- **American Board of Professional Psychology (ABPP)** – certification board for thirteen different specialties in psychology
- **National Association of State Boards of Education** – provides information on public policy, current issues, professional standards and ethics.

Civil liabilities: "standard of care", sexual misconduct, illegal search and seizure, defamation, breach of contract, copyright infringement

Criminal liabilities: accessory after the fact, failure to report child abuse, contributing to the delinquency of a minor, sexual misconduct.

Accessory after the fact:
    Felony committed
    Knowledge of felony
    Harboring felon (or shielding)

Ethics constitute a body of moral principles and values. Ethical standards have been developed by professional organizations as guidelines for membership practices (i.e. American Counseling Association's Code of Ethics & Standard Practices can be located at http://www.counseling.org).

As professionals, individuals must ensure:

1. That their *documentation* meets the highest professional standards.
   a. Professional Documentation is legal documentation and as such there is a responsibility to create and maintain documents in detail and quality that would be consistent with reasonable scrutiny in adjudication.
   b. Professional Documentation:
      i. must facilitate provision of services at a later date by any professional
      ii. must ensure accountability
      iii. must meet the requirements of the institution, the regulatory agencies and the law.
2. That the standards of *confidentiality* are upheld.
   a. Limits of Confidentiality
      i. Child Protective Services Laws
      ii. legal
      iii. terms of probation
      iv. subpoenaed by the courts
      v. age of consent / parental rights
      vi. treatment team disclosure
      vii. harm to self or others
   b. Maintaining Confidentiality
      i. of documentation
      ii. of conversation
      iii. of records
      iv. of client identity
   c. Confidentiality and Intrusion of Privacy Issues
      i. family members
      ii. for curiosity sake
      iii. without consent
      iv. HIPAA – medical information
   d. Confidentiality and Storage of Records
      i. client charts
      ii. professional communication logs
      iii. shift reports
      iv. incident or accident reports
   e. Confidentiality and Disclosures
      i. release of information must contain
         1. signature
         2. specific identification of information forms to be released
         3. time limited
      ii. third party information cannot be released even with an Informed Consent / Release of Information (information not generated by your organization, even if this information is part of the client record i.e. copies of public school records for a client in an outpatient treatment setting)

        iii. verification of identity is required
             1. for facsimile transmissions (Fax number should be verified and a confidentiality statement should be included on the fax face sheet)
             2. personal communication of information
             3. phone communication of information
             4. mailing records requires the verification of the address and envelopes and records should be stamped "Confidential"

3. That clients and families are treated with dignity and respect. Professional boundaries must be established and maintained so that *relationships* among counselors, clients and families facilitate positive growth and development.
4. *Professional Relationships:*
   a. Relationships involve at least two individuals; often with different viewpoints of the extent of the relationship.
   b. The perception of the relationship can be more important than the reality of the relationship.
   c. Be aware of the potential for harm
   d. Be aware of the potential for treatment interference
   e. Involve a danger of exploitation
   f. Professional should set relationship limits.
      i. If you are uncomfortable at any point:
      ii. Seek supervision
      iii. Talk with members of your team
      iv. Talk to the client in a controlled, supervised and supportive environment
5. That they maintain their *boundaries of competence*.
   a. *Limits of Competence:* Professionals must recognize the limits of their competence and perform only those services for which they have been trained.
   b. All staff must abide by the *Agency/Organizational Policies & Procedures*.
   c. *Boundaries of Competence:* Know your skill level and level of expertise (certifications, licensees, training) and remain within the boundaries of your competency.
   d. To develop and maintain skills and qualifications, professionals are encouraged to seek:
      i. Training
      ii. Education
      iii. Research and Studies
      iv. Supervision
      v. Experience

Critical Ethical Issues in Professional Practice:
1. AIDS counseling
2. Family counseling
3. Working with students
4. Sex therapy
5. Counseling with gays and lesbians
6. Group counseling, generally
7. Liability, insurance
8. Counselor's role during search and seizure
9. Student educational files
10. Romantic relationships with clients
11. Ethics and law
12. ADA-employment discrimination
13. Sexual harassment
14. Risk management

TO DO!
Activities:

#1 Identify and explain the trends that influence the need for your Change Effort

_____

_____

#2 Identify the declining resources that influence the need for your Change Effort.

#3 List the ethical issues critical to your Change Effort.

#4 Identify advocacy groups and/or existing advisory boards that may be of assistance to your Change Effort. Explain the importance of advocacy groups and/or existing advisory boards to the Change Effort. Identify contact information for these advocacy groups and/or existing advisory boards.

#5 Identify new technologies that may affect your Change Effort.

#6 List the three types of disclosure and provide examples of how you would meet these requirements for your Change Effort.

#7 Explain the Ethical implications of the following anonymous anecdote:
Worst thing that can happen to a youngster starting school," said the lawyer, "is to be caught cheating." "Not at all," said the clergyman, "the worst thing at the start of a person's life is to cheat and not get caught."

Key terms and Concepts: Can you define and explain each of the following key terms? Are you prepared to offer brief examples or applicable context for each concept?

Accessory After the Fact:

Agency Disclosure:

Boundaries of Competence:

Child Protective Service Laws:

Civil Liability:

Code of Ethics:

_____

_____

Collective Power:

_____

_____

Consumer Disclosure:

_____

_____

Criminal Liability:

_____

_____

Declining Resources:

_____

_____

Discrimination:

_____

_____

Duty to Warn:

_____

_____

Ethical Standards:

_____

_____

Informed Consent:

_____

_____

Intrusion of Privacy:

_____

_____

Legal Obligations:

_____

_____

Need for Change:

_____

_____

Privileged Communication:

_____

_____

Professional Relationship:

_____

_____

Public Disclosure:

_____
_____

Release of Information:

_____
_____

Service Quality Review:

_____
_____

Tarasoff vs. Regents:

_____
_____

Third Party Information:

_____
_____

Questions:

Name and explain 4 trends influencing need to change.
Describe the primary difference between civil liability and criminal liability.
Name and explain the four key points of privileged communication.

Chronicle and Rumination:

This is the space provided to _CHRONICLE_ your thoughts and to _RUMINATE_ over the material presented in this chapter along with the references, outside readings, classroom activities, and experiences. Documenting your thoughts and feelings will provide a written account of your _Effective Planning Strategies and Proposal Writing_ education.

Chapter 7
Resource Planning

Chapter Outcomes: At the completion of this chapter, activities and assignments, the student will:
1. Identify and explain types of funders
2. Understand three types of budgets
3. Understand and create a budget for Change Effort

Overview:
Trends are the driving force behind funding for Change Efforts. It is important for Change Agents and organizations not to try to make the funder/grantor's program fit what you want to do. The Change Effort must be in line with the funding source's priorities. Preparing the financial plan for a Change Effort requires investigation into three areas: the resources needed for the change effort (broken down into individual expenditures and tasks), the policies of your agency/organization, and the requirements of the funding source and/or RFP. The Budget Types (Zero-based, Formula, and Incremental) and funding sources (private and public) will vary depending on the type of Change Effort developed. Generally, grant funders expect to see a Zero-based, line-item budget embedded into the overall Resource Plan.

Quintessence: Trends drive money allocations.
Funding types (2):
1. Public funders – government or public monies (tax dollars) /oriented toward social trends (i.e. National Institute of Health)
2. Private funders – foundations/ usually have an agenda/follow trends identified by the board or chairperson

Resource Plan
1. Budget is a forecast of all cash/financial sources and cash expenditures
    a. Zero-based, line-item budget: is to justify budget requests every budgeting cycle, regardless of prior budget period outcomes.
        The zero-based, line-item budgeting system puts the burden of proof on the change agent for justifying the entire budget in detail and rationalization for spending the organizations or funders money. Development of a Zero-based, line-item budget requires: analysis of cost, purpose, alternative course of action, measures of performance, consequences for not performing the activity, and the benefits (differing from traditional budgets due to the analysis of alternatives). A zero-based budget assumes that the budgeting process begins with no funds (0) and builds upward as need for funding is demonstrated.

EXAMPLE:

Zero-based, line-item budget for Enhanced Parenting Skill Program 2009-2010

Category	Amount Requested	Matching Funds	Total (B & C)
Occupancy (rent, utilities)	$2,000.00	$1,600.00	$3,600.00
Printed Materials	$500.00		$500.00
Office Supplies	$1,700.00		$1,700.00

Program Supplies	$6200.00	$3,100.00	$9,300.00
Child Care for Participants	$400.00	$400.00	$800.00
Telephone	$600.00		$600.00
Liability Insurance		$2000.00	$2000.00
Seminars, Travel	$3000.00		$3000.00
Social, Presenter	$1,800.00		$1,800.00
Foster Parents' Per Diems	$36,440.00		$36,440.00
Client Transport	$3,000.00		$3,000.00
Administrative overhead 7.5%	$8650.00		$8,650.00
Total Operating	$64,290.00	$7,100.00	$71,390.00
Grand Total (Personnel & Operating)	$123,290.00	$7,100.00	$130,390.00

b. Formula – based on a pre-established formula or percentage (%) of total budget allocation (i.e. state student educational reimbursement rates). Budgeting methods of allocating funds based on needs and population can promote greater resource equity (common categories for weighting educational funds include: population, special education, poverty, limited English proficiency, vocational, and gifted education). While formula budgets may sound fair and equable in the distribution of funds, they do not always take into account individual differences and all contributing needs. From this perspective Formula budgets can sharply reduce public services, impair ability to respond to needs, federal mandates, and changing circumstances (i.e. severity of the population, population growth within a budget cycle, federal or state mandates such as "No Child Left Behind"). The formula has generally been developed by the funder. Often a simple pie-chart provides an illustration of formula budgeting, with "pieces of the pie" adding up to 100% (one whole pie) of funding. Formulas are generally based upon a historically sound rationale—population trends, as example—however, they are often unresponsive to change. The bigger pieces of the original "pie" dislike getting smaller.

EXAMPLE:

Student-based Formula Budgeting

Actual School X dollar expenditures   =   District-weighted average
Student-weighted index for School X   expenditures for school X
            (The actual reimbursement per student is determined by this formula.)

c. Incremental budget – is prepared using a previous period's budget allotment or actual performance as a basis, with incremental amounts/percentages added for the new budget period (start with last funding period amount of $ as a bottom line). The allocation of resources is based on allocations from the previous budget period. This approach does not take into account changes in circumstances and encourages "spending up to the budget" to ensure reasonable allocations in the next budget period (spend it or lose it mentality). Advantages include a stable budget with gradual change, consistent operating budget, and easy observation of impact.

EXAMPLE:

Incremental budget
(Budget years Two and Three are based on a projected 3.5% annual increase from the funding source)

Operating Expenses:				
	Year 1	Year 2	Adj.%	Totals - 3 Year period
Advertising	$3,200.00	$3.680.00	15%	$10.928.00
Depreciation	$4,000.00	$4200.00	5%	$12,610.00
Insurance	$1,700.00	$1,732.00	2%	$5,198.68
Legal & Accounting	$3,400.00	$3,570.00	5%	$10,718.50

Office expenses	$2,200.00	$2288.00	4%	$6,867.52
Rent	$24,000.00	$24,000.00	0%	$72,000.00
Repair & Maintenance	$300.00	$318.00	6%	$955.08
Salaries	$33,000.00	$34,320.00	4%	$103,012.80
Employee Benefits	$5,610.00	$5,834.40	4%	$17,512.18
Utilities	$6,000.00	$6,600.00	10%	$19,860.00
Misc.	$920.00	$782.00	-15%	$2,484.00
Total operating expenses	$84,330.00	$87,324.40	3.5%	$262,138.76

2. Include indirects and matching funds – no real monies are exchanged, but can provide a source of income for a nonprofit agency. Can be a percentage calculated from an existing employee's salary, work time, effort, or benefits. Utilities, space rental, and contracted services/consultation can also be used for indirects/match.
3. Legal fees can be built in separately or in conjunction with consultation expenses.

The overall Resource Plan may include narrative to address all resource needs, unless those needs can be accounted for within the other funding source columns of the Budget, itself.

TO DO!

Activities:

#1 Explain the Strengths and Liabilities to using each Budget Type with your specific Change Effort.

Zero-Based Budget:

Strengths:

_____
_____
_____

Liabilities:

_____
_____
_____

Formula-Based Budget:

Strengths:

_____
_____
_____

Liabilities:

_____
_____
_____

Incremental Budget:

Strengths:

_____
_____
_____

Liabilities:

_____

#2   Create a Zero-based, line-item budget for your Change Effort.

> **INSTRUCTIONS:** Applicant to insert entries on the "Proposed Expenditures" line under each appropriate heading *ROUNDING FIGURES*: ALL AMOUNTS MUST BE ROUNDED TO THE NEAREST DOLLAR FOR BUDGETING PURPOSES.

Key terms and Concepts: Can you define and explain each of the following key terms? Are you prepared to offer brief examples or applicable context for each concept?

Public Funders:

_____
_____

Private Funders:

_____
_____

Resource Plan:

_____
_____

Zero-based, line-item Budget:

_____
_____

Formula-based Budget:

_____
_____

Incremental-based Budget:

_____
_____

Indirects:

_____
_____

Matching Funds:

_____
_____

Consultants:

_____
_____

Questions:

Explain the differences among the three types of budgets.

List four examples of indirect and matching funds.

Chronicle and Rumination:

This is the space provided to *Chronicle* your thoughts and to *Ruminate* over the material presented in this chapter along with the references, outside readings, classroom activities, and experiences. Documenting your thoughts and feelings will provide a written account of your *Effective Planning Strategies and Proposal Writing* education.

Chapter 8
External Funding

Chapter Outcomes: At the completion of this chapter, activities and assignments, the student will:
1. Identify and explain national trends in funding
2. Identify and develop funding sources/resources for Change Effort
3. Investigate funding sources to determine criteria and qualifications for application of funds
4. Identify Key factors that link a funding source to an identified Change Effort

Overview:

Funding sources can be categorized as *public* (including local, state, and federal funds – tax dollars) and *private* (including foundations, corporations, special interest groups, etc.). Acquiring and accessing these funds requires research and planning. It is important for Change Agents and organizations not to try to make the funder /grantor's program fit what you want to do – the Change Effort must be in line with the funding source's priorities.

Preparing the financial plan for a Change Effort requires investigation into three areas: the resources needed for the change effort (broken down into individual expenditures and tasks), the policies of your agency/organization, and the requirements of the funding source and/or RFP. The relationship between your proposed effort and the funding source initiatives must be clear.

Quintessence: Funding types (2):
1. Public funders – government or public monies (tax dollars) oriented toward social trends i.e. National Institute of Health. Tax dollars may come from local, state, or federal sources.
2. Private funders – foundations and private parties usually have an agenda. Trends are identified by the board or chairperson (from foundations, corporations, special interest groups, etc.)

In general, external funds emerge directly from national trends. Recent trends significantly influencing the helping professions have included the following:
1. Working with special populations (DSM-IV-TR diagnosed; economically-disadvantaged; those experiencing marginalization due to age, race, gender, religious preference, sexual orientation, etc)
2. Accountability - assessment of needs and evidence of outcomes/related data
3. Reductions in funds – due to a decreased confidence in the helping professions among the tax-paying public and an aging population with different priorities (no longer have children in school/not interesting in funding school programs)
4. Increase in the need for external funds – grant monies to support professional development and programs
5. Increased competition for funding among helping professions and related agencies
6. Technology – advancing technology in education and social services

Related to national trends impacting the helping professions and opportunities for external funding, public confidence (at an all-time low), organizational and external "politics", and the overall challenge of "managing it all" have to be taken into consideration. Private and public funders are both influenced by these trends and considerations.

Public Funders

In spite of the need for external funds, many public funds remain untapped. Unlike private funds, access to public funding is primarily determined by the strength of a proposal in documenting a local need that is clearly linked to the funder's primary initiative(s).

Although the change agent must demonstrate interaction with various people to the satisfaction of the public funder, a poorly-written proposal will typically not be countered effectively by the "people skills" of the change agent. A listing of information for public sources is provided at the end of this book.

Private Funders
In general, private funders tend to fund "people". These funders are more likely to fund your initiative after they express approval of your presentation of yourself than as a result of a fine proposal you have submitted. Once impressed, they more frequently request a written submission.

Typically, private funders must be encountered face-to-face. Opportunities for these exchanges may occur in many ways, including fund-raising events, foundation meetings, etc. Previously funded change agents can provide insight into the "how-to's" for a particular funder. A list of information for private sources is provided at the end of this book.

What if one funder cannot provide adequate funds for your effort?
It is not unusual for a change effort to require funding from more than one funder in order to meet the goals and objectives—and accompanying methods/activities—for the change effort. Funders accept these realities and typically expect only that the change agent will account for all funders within the proposed Resource Plan.

Change agents can account for specific funds from each funder through separate Budget columns or through narrative within the Resource Plan.

Example #1: Budget Column Approach

Property Acquisition for Expanded Parking Facilities Change Effort	National Science Foundation Requested Funds	Total
Purchase of property	$225,000.00	$225,000.00
Lot improvements [signage, curbing, drainage, and paving]	$50,000.00	$50,000.00
Yearly increased operational costs [taxes, snow removal, greens upkeep & repairs]	$2,000.00	$2,000.00
Total for Budget	$275,000.00	$275,000.00

Example #2: Narrative Approach

All Budget lines refer to funding being requested through your foundation. Other funds required for services described in the Methods section of this proposal, including property and utilities, will be provided by the stated education association (see their allocation in Appendix C).

TO DO!

Activities:

#1 For your Change Effort, identify at least two possible funding sources from each of the following categories:

Private Sector (corporate or special interest groups:

_____

_____

Public Sector:

_____

_____

#2 Identify contact information for each identified funding source listed above.

_____

_____

_____
_____
_____

#3 Investigate at least one of the possible funding sources to identify the criteria/qualifications for applying for the funds.

_____
_____
_____
_____
_____

#4 Identify the key factors that link these possible funding sources to your Change Effort.

_____
_____
_____
_____
_____

Key terms and Concepts: Can you define and explain each of the following key terms? Are you prepared to offer brief examples or applicable context for each concept?

Accountability:
_____
_____

External Funds:
_____
_____

Foundations:
_____
_____

Outcome Measures:
_____
_____

Private Sector:
_____
_____

Public Sector:
_____
_____

Technology:
_____
_____

Trends:
_____
_____

Questions:

What key words or phrases would you use for an internet search to locate possible funding sources for your Change Effort?
What Library sources would you use to locate possible funding sources for you Change Effort?

_____
_____
_____
_____

Chronicle and Rumination:

This is the space provided to *chronicle* your thoughts and to *ruminate* over the material presented in this chapter along with the references, outside readings, classroom activities, and experiences. Documenting your thoughts and feelings will provide a written account of your *Effective Planning Strategies and Proposal Writing* education.

_____
_____
_____
_____
_____
_____
_____
_____
_____
_____
_____
_____
_____
_____
_____
_____
_____
_____
_____
_____
_____
_____

Chapter 9
Effective Leadership

Chapter Outcomes: At the completion of this chapter, activities and assignments, the student will:

1. Identify and explain methods for small group techniques
2. Identify motivational techniques for presentation of Change Effort
3. Understand leadership styles
4. Identify and explain development of personal leadership style
5. Understand the aspects of groupthink
6. Identify your own leadership preferences
7. Develop an organizational chart
8. Identify and explain a small group techniques used to develop ideas for a mission statement for your Change Effort, including the following:
   a. Identify and explain a small group technique used to develop success criteria for your Change Effort.
   b. Understand and explain the dynamics of conflict in groups
      i. Identify criteria for effective implementation, compliance, performance
      ii. Understand how to set the action plan into action
      iii. Understand how to effectively manage conflict and resistance
      iv. Determine how to strengthen the support base for a change effort

Overview:

Leadership and *organizational structure* play significant roles in the planning process. In this section, Leadership Styles and Approaches are explored in relationship to organizational structure and administrative oversight methods. Small group techniques are also pivotal to successful planning. This chapter highlights: Brainstorming Methods, SWOT Analysis, Delphi Techniques, Focus Groups, Collecting Post-Its, Nominal Group Techniques, Critical Incident Techniques/Debriefing, Steps in Principled Negotiation and Conflict Management Techniques.

Quintessence: Effective Leadership/Effective Planning

Elements of Effective Planning:

1. Utilization of a planning team and/or advisory board
   a. Reasons for using a planning team/advisory board
      i. can assist in planning from start to finish
      ii. can be especially helpful in accessing populations for needs assessments
      iii. can help minimize future conflict/manage obstacles
      iv. can generate creative ideas
      v. can assist with *force-field analysis*
      vi. can be effective source of volunteers

b. Composition of a planning team/advisory board
   i. should include potential restraining forces (people who might try to hinder your success)
   ii. should include potential facilitating forces (people who are not directly responsible for your success but could have a negative impact, if not included)
   iii. should include potential driving forces (people who are in positions of power who can ensure success)
   iv. should include members of target population
   v. should include others, as appropriate
   vi. should not be unwieldy in size (consider no more than 10 to 12)
   vii. should include constituencies mandates for grant funds

2. Conducting planning analyses
   a. Force-field analyses (before team composed and after, with team input)
   b. Organizational structure
      i. Leadership style: classifies how a leader leads, rather than why an individual becomes a leader. There are three styles of leadership, identified as Authoritarian, Democratic, and Laissez-faire
         1. Authoritarian – the leader leads with firm control and takes on the responsibility of decision-making process
         2. Democratic – the leader recognizes the group value and encourages participation in discussion, processes, and decision-making
         3. Laissez-faire – the leader takes on the role of a group member, allowing the group to lead itself. This leadership style operates from a "hands-off" approach and the leader does not exert or enforce the leader position in the decision-making process
      ii. Functional leadership approach: views leadership in light of the communication behaviors of any group member that leads the group toward the identified goal; the process is central rather than the skills or traits. The Functional leadership approach focuses on individual actions that affect the task and social aspects of the group that facilitate goal attainment.
      iii. Situational leadership approach: identifies the characteristics for effective leadership based upon the specific situation. In the Situational approach, the group determines the central requirements of the situation and determines what type of leadership style and personality would be most effective to realize the group goals. Ultimately, the individual's knowledge and experience are most useful in determining who emerges as the leader, in a given situation.
      iv. Trait leadership approach: proposes that individuals are born with specific personality traits that control their ability to become good leaders. These characteristics include both physical and personality traits. The Trait approach is based on characteristics that the individual is born with, supporting the phrase, "born leader". This approach to leadership has not been substantiated as a successful determinate of leadership qualities
      v. Task and Maintenance orientations
      vi. Agency's mission; effort goals and objectives, as well as where within either the existing structure or within a newly-created structure the proposed initiative would be housed
   c. Antecedent conditions (include all above)
      i. residue from past change efforts
      ii. organizational effort(s) toward planning, to date

3. Demonstrating need: a gap between what you have and what you want
   a. Organizational "mindset" is needed for change—in reviewing the organizational structure, it is critical that the proposed initiative be housed within a unit that would be appropriate to the change and enhance its potential for "success".
   b. Review of the organization's mission and its relevance to the proposed initiative is periodically needed.
   c. Mission statements should relate to present-day "reality", as well to what is likely for the "future".
   d. Is there an organizational mindset that: "working smarter" is better than "working harder"?
   e. Change is based on the realities of the future, not just present factors.
   f. Efforts are made to create the future that is needed, not just the one that exists.

4. Motivating to action through the development of issues (get people doing something or doing something differently to make things better)
   a. Highlight aspects of the issue that make people **feel**:
      i. angry
      ii. guilty
      iii. excited
      iv. or other strong emotion
   b. Challenge people with the issue, showing how it puts something they value on the line or provides a test.

c. Increase discomfort with the present situation by emphasizing the negative side of the issue. Present the irritating details of the harmful consequences of current conditions.
d. Rub the sores of discontent, using the issues to prod and poke at the things with which people are frustrated.

Change Agent Tip		
Once a group is really rolling with their litany of complaints, you want to get them to think about acting to make things different. A few key comments can turn the conversation from impotent frustration toward action. Essentially, you want to get the group to focus on a choice between hanging onto their frustrating situation or acting to make it different. There are many different things you can say to	change the direction of the conversation. The point is to keep your comments or questions short. Some examples are: * I guess we could hang onto being so frustrated or we could do something. Which should we do? * Now that we have gotten all this off our chests, are we going to just sit back and let things stay the same?	* It feels good to finally get this all off our chests, doesn't it? Maybe it feels so good that we can keep meeting like this without ever doing anything to make things different. *I don't suppose we actually want to do anything about this? *Sounds like we are ready to make some changes around here. * Where can we start making changes?

5. Models of Administrative Oversight
   a. Chain of Command: reporting is designed up a identified (single unit per level) chain of command, based on knowing to whom you report
   b. Institutional Officers: reporting is through an institutional officer, a number of people report to the institutional officer; this individual is responsible for the decision making (institutional officer generally reports to the Chief Executive Officer or the Board of Directors)
   c. Dual Reporting Model: two identified parties to report to; can cause confusion and conflicts when conflicting directives or expectations are presented
   d. Decentralized organizational structure: separate units without centralized oversight (compare to anarchy), difficult to plan
6. Elements of Strategic Planning
   a. **Effective Brainstorming Method**
      i. Before
         1. define purpose
         2. choose a few participants (5-8)
         3. change environment
         4. design informal atmosphere
         5. choose facilitator
      ii. During
         1. seat participants side-by-side, facing the problem
         2. clarify ground rules; no criticism of others' ideas
         3. brainstorm, listing ALL ideas
         4. record ideas in full view of entire group
      iii. After
         1. star (highlight) most promising ideas
         2. invent improvements for promising ideas
         3. set up time frame to evaluate ideas and decide on course of action
      iv. Additional tips
         1. what if one side is more powerful? Look for best alternative strategy and whether or not you have a bottom line.
         2. what if one side won't play by the rules? Don't attack this issue; look at what's behind the rule breaking.
         3. invite criticism and advice.
         4. recast an attack on you as an attack on the problem.
         5. use effective questioning and pausing.
   b. **SWOT** Analysis
      i. **S)** – Strengths
      ii. **W)** – Weaknesses
      iii. **O)** – Opportunity
      iv. **T)** – Threats
      v. Tasks

      1. scoping:
         a. Who are the consumers?
         b. Who benefits from change?
      2. data collecting:
         a. What are our goals?
         b. Do we have objectives toward meeting those goals that are result-oriented and measurable?
         c. What are the needs?
      3. planning:
         a. Does the organization (structure, leadership, etc.) match with the mission/goals/objectives?
         b. What should we do about mismatches and can we reconcile differences. Or do we need to do some "housekeeping" or make "moves"?
         c. Are we future-oriented?
         d. What are the SWOT's?
      4. implementing and evaluating

c. **Delphi Technique**
    i. Planning team is identified
    ii. An "enquirer" is identified (is not and will not be part of actual effort)
    iii. Ideas and feedback are anonymously collected from team members by the enquirer
    iv. Enquirer is responsible to collect, summarize and distribute responses
    v. Planning team members review the summaries and respond again
    vi. Process continues in a "brainstorming" manner with anonymity
    vii. Final composite is distributed before the next team meeting, when open discussion can occur
    viii. Team places much confidence in the **enquirer**.

d. **Focus Group**
    i. Techniques similar to brainstorming except information is distributed to team members/participants in advance of an actual meeting
        1. identified target
        2. focus questions
        3. issues for discussion
    ii. Facilitator/change agent summarizes responses
    iii. Group examines the already summarized responses and processes
        1. combining
        2. deleting
        3. prioritizing of ideas

e. **Collecting Post-Its**
    i. Planning team may or may not have received materials in advance
    ii. Summary responses are written on newsprint around the meeting room (or on chalk board/dry-erase board)
    iii. Team members are given post-its to write responses to themes and are instructed to place post-it comments under the summarized headings around the room
        1. eliminates the need for a recorder
        2. allows for a number of responses in a short time period
        3. team members can remain somewhat anonymous

f. **Nominal Group Technique**
    i. Planning team goes through a brainstorming process
    ii. Team members vote on their favorite ideas

g. **Critical Incident Technique**
    i. Approach is similar to a "de-briefing"
    ii. Often used after a change episode; but before implementation with the target population
    iii. Planning team identifies what they believe to be the most important outputs from the target population (this may be accomplished through the use of any small group technique)
    iv. After implementation these critical outputs are identified on an evaluation that is given to the target population
    v. Team reconvenes to identify if the target population identified the most important areas (did the target population "get it"?)

Common Errors in Planning
1. Not thinking "big enough
2. Objectives were not result-oriented
3. Input was not solicited and/or used from key forces
4. Change agent assumed he/she had the solution beforehand (as in researcher bias)
5. Change agent and/or team set objectives solely on their own perceptions
6. Assumption that helping professionals' planning occurs best at the intuitive level
7. Change agent and/or team did not think through all of the components in planning before beginning

Leadership Inventories:
- www.questia.com
- www.MySkillsProfile.com
- www.coastal.com
- www.360facilitated.com
- www.360facilitated.com/crystal/freetools.cfm
- www.psyww.com/resource/bytopic/testing.html

Force field analysis - Kurt Lewin – people forces: 3 types
1. *Potential restraining force:* people who might try to hinder your success – to get them on board with the effort
2. *Potential driving force:* people who are in positions of power who can ensure success of effort
3. *Potential facilitating force:* people who are not directly responsible for your success but who could have a negative impact if not included

Approaches to Profiling Leaders:
1. Trait: innate / born with the ability to lead
2. Styles: (traditional approach) – how a leader leads
   a. Democratic – majority rules (always an unhappy "camper" in minority group)
   b. Authoritarian – decision maker (works best during times when "heroics" are necessary)
   c. Laissez-faire – allows the group to lead itself (assumes much maturity on part of group)
3. Functional: focused on group process
   a. Task – content – what we have to do to get the job done
   b. Maintenance – additional tasks to accomplish the task – process to get others to get the job done
4. Situational/Transformational (*In Search of Excellence*) – can change and motivate to get the job done
5. Energies: "combination" approach – we are all leaders but put energy into different areas
   Glanz (2002) identifies 3 primary leadership energies:
   a. Dynamic energy: personal magnetism that inspires others
   b. Adaptive energy: personal need to lead less than energy toward accommodating
   c. Creative energy: personal rhythm and awareness toward new ideas

In the energies approach to leadership, all energy "types" provide significance to the change effort. Glanz also describes three secondary energies:
   Aggressive: energy toward control.
   Assertive: energy toward change
   Supportive: energy toward communication
The combination of energies provides even more opportunities to describe and understand the uniqueness of individuals in "leading" with a change effort.

5 steps to principled negotiation:
   a. Separate the people from the problem (Delphi technique)
   b. Focus on the interests, not the positions
   c. Generate a variety of possibilities before deciding what to do (brainstorming)
   d. Insist that the results be based on objective standards
   e. Act

3 Approaches:	Making Change	Surviving Change	Organic Change
Focus of Change	Forcing or driving change by positional power. Organization is insular and change comes from within – top down change.	Surviving change that is forced upon us from external forces. Scanning environment is added to strategically protect and respond to outside threats.	Influencing the system through organic strategies. Increase ability to respond quickly to change. Intentional multi-directional influencing.
Organization Values	Predictable and controlled change. Long range goals. Buying into organizational goals.	Increasing organizational capacity to survive. Constantly adjusting to environmental conditions. Do more with less. Crisis management training.	Develop strategic partnerships.
Meaning Making	Found in predictable patterns, staying on purpose; clear picture of result; if we accomplish this change we will succeed.	Found in threats and opportunities that emerge as patterns in larger environment, belief that we can survive this.	Found in relational thinking; belief that collective intelligence and innovations will lead to new ways of influencing the system.

Animal styles in conflict management (symbolism):
1. Turtle: withdrawn, seething
2. Shark: aggressive, damaging relationships
3. Teddy bear: needs to please, approval needs, questionable credibility
4. Fox: bright, clever, negotiating style, gets dumped on
5. Owl: works toward a consensus, not a compromise

Political pressure tactics:
1. Mobilizing a crowd
2. Prepared statement for public hearing
3. Signed petitions
4. 1:1 lobbying
5. Letter campaigns
6. Phone calls, emails
7. Suggesting the wording of the law
8. Attending a rule-making session

Group Think:
1. Too cohesive
2. Gang mentality

5 conditions of group think:
1. Reach a high level of cohesiveness
2. Shared perceptions of "can do no wrong"
3. Isolated from feedback outside the group
4. Dissention within the group is prohibited
5. Lack of impartial leadership discourages members from questioning the group

Four ways to prevent group think
1. Leader should stress critical thinking
2. Seek outside feedback
3. Assign a devil's advocate
4. Invite outside observation

Guided Decision Making: every group member is a group leader

Guided Behavior Skills:
1. Requesting information
2. Providing information
3. Clarifying information

4. Guiding discussion
5. Summarizing
6. Analyzing and reasoning
7. Negotiating

Conflict is a struggle or disagreement between two or more options or people; can be more internal than external.

MYTHS about Conflict:
1. Avoid conflict at all costs
2. Conflict is always someone else's fault
3. All conflict can be resolved

Caring for yourself:
1. Leave some things to others
2. Leave your ego at the door
3. Leave time for other things
4. Leave the paddle at home
5. Leave room to learn

Functional small groups:
1. Coalitions – groups formed around a narrow issue, group formation by participants (can also end up being problematic, if a "groupthink" mentality evolves)
2. Ad hoc – formed to address a limited issue, this group has knowledge of the "big picture" and the group is formed for a specific purpose (not limited to experts)
3. Task force – temporary group of people with expertise
4. Networking – the formation of connections with other individuals or groups to advance individual or group goals

Organizational Accreditations
Organizational Accreditations provide a standard by which agencies/organizations are evaluated. These accreditations provide the consumer with the assurance that the agency/organization has met the proficiency in defined standards to obtain this accreditation. Obtaining and maintaining accreditation does not mean completing a checklist of qualification. Accrediting Boards evaluate an agency/organization on their processes. These are ongoing practices that involve Needs Assessment, Purposeful Planning, Implementation of Action Plans, Formative Evaluation, and the development of Policies and Procedures; all of which are designed to ensure Quality Improvement within the agency/organization.

Examples of accrediting boards:
- **Joint Commission on Accreditation of Health Organizations (JCAHO)** – accredits hospitals and health care providers including mental health agencies and programs
- **Council for Accreditation of Counseling & Related Educational Programs (CACREP)** - accredits career, geriatric, marriage & family, mental health/community, and school counseling programs, plus doctoral programs in professional counseling research/teaching/clinical supervision (a.k.a. "counselor education"), in the U.S.; has an on-line directory of accredited programs; an affiliate of the American Counseling Assoc.
- **Council on Rehabilitation Education (CORE)** - accredits rehabilitation counseling programs in the U.S.; has an on-line directory of accredited programs

TO DO!

#1 Write a brief essay explaining your leadership style and how it developed (one to three pages).

#2 Develop an Organization Chart for your Change Effort

#3 Identify three motivational techniques for presentation of your Change Effort

_____
_____
_____
_____
_____

#4 Provide an example of groupthink and explain how you would counteract this issue, linking your actions to your identified leadership style.

_____
_____
_____
_____
_____

#5 To what leadership style do you respond best? Why?

_____
_____
_____
_____
_____

#6 Identify the leadership style that is most difficult for you to respond to, in a supervisor. Why?

_____
_____
_____
_____
_____

#7 Identify the leadership style of each of your parents and explain your response to the leadership/parenting style.

_____
_____
_____
_____
_____

Key terms and Concepts: Can you define and explain each of the following key terms? Are you prepared to offer brief examples or applicable context for each concept?

Change Episode:

_____
_____

Force-Field Analysis:

_____
_____

Restraining Forces:

_____
_____

Facilitation Forces:

_____
_____

Driving Forces:

_____
_____

Target Population:

_____
_____

Democratic Leadership Style:

_____
_____

Laissez-faire Leadership Style:

_____
_____

Authoritarian Leadership Style:

_____
_____

Situational Leadership Style:

_____
_____

Antecedent Conditions:

_____
_____

Demonstration of Need:

_____
_____

Mission:

_____
_____

SWOT analysis:

_____
_____

Delphi Technique:

_____
_____

Focus Group Technique:

_____
_____

Nominal Group Technique:

_____
_____

Critical Incident Technique:

_____
_____

Questions:

What small group techniques could you use to develop ideas for a mission statement for your Change Effort? Explain
What small group technique could you use to establish success criteria for your Change Effort? Explain

_____
_____
_____
_____
_____
_____

Chronicle and Rumination:

This is the space provided to *chronicle* your thoughts and to *ruminate* over the material presented in this chapter along with the references, outside readings, classroom activities, and experiences. Documenting your thoughts and feelings will provide a written account of your *Effective Planning Strategies and Proposal Writing* education.

Chapter Ten
Reassessment and Stabilization

Chapter Outcomes: At the completion of this chapter, activities and assignments, the student will:
1. Identify tasks of reassessing and stabilizing a completed change effort cycle.
   a. Delineate factors determining continuation/discontinuation of the effort
   b. Delineate factors determining future role of change agent
   c. Identify and explain the components of evaluation
2. Develop reassessment and stabilization methods and establish criteria for Change Effort.
3. Develop evaluating criteria and/or questions to assess the Change Agent's performance/role in the Change Effort.
4. Develop evaluating criteria and/or questions to assess the Team's performance/role in the Change Effort.
5. Identify and explain the five major roles of a Change Agent

Overview:

With the development of the goals, objectives and methods, the change agent needs to develop the evaluation process and determine what will constitute the success or failure of the change effort. The process of evaluation includes assessment of the effectiveness and the efficiency of the project as they relate to: effort or activities, performance or outcomes, adequacy of performance, efficiency (cost), and implementation (action plan) process. Reassessment addresses the evaluative characteristics and stabilization addresses continuation conditions of the project.

Quintessence: Reassessment and Stabilization (bringing change episode to closure)
   Requirements:
      1. Input from participants
      2. Reflection on meaning
      3. Timing
      4. Momentum
      5. Readiness
      6. Acceptance and approval
      7. Closure
   Models of Evaluation
      1. Needs Assessment – is conducted before the change effort begins, as an investigative tool to determine the gap between what you have and what you want.
      2. Feasibility Study – is conducted during the design of the change effort, to examine alternatives and the probability of the success for this project.

Example:

Feasibility Study Budget

Expense	Quantity	Cost per unit	Total
Olszak Management Consulting, Inc.			$15,640.00
Roundtable Meeting Expenses	10	$300.00	$3,000.00
Travel Expenses – Interviews			$1,000.00
Books / Materials / Supplies			$360.00
Total Project Costs			$20,000.00

Revenues			
McCune Foundation Grant – Projected			$15,640.00
Bethesda Children's Home - Matching Funds			$4,360.00
Total Revenues			$20,000.00

3. Process Evaluation – (formative evaluation) is conducted during the change effort to track the implementation progression and project alterations/adaptations. Monitoring the effort is significant because it allows the change agent to modify content, personnel—even budget lines—in a timely manner. If requesting budgetary changes, the change agent petitions the funder(s) through submission of a change letter. It should be noted that some line items may not be permitted to be modified. Funders refer to these as "fixed costs". Change agents need to be aware of these items.
4. Outputs/Outcomes Evaluation – (summative evaluation) is conducted at the end of the change effort or a change effort cycle, to determine if the change effort goals and objectives have been met satisfactorily; can also be used to determine the need or feasibility for continuation of the change effort, the discontinuation of the change effort or modifications to the change effort (will the change effort continue, be modified, be duplicated, or be terminated). Most funders expect to review summative data that measures initial gains among the target population (outputs) and gains maintained over time (outcomes).
5. Cost Analysis – (summative evaluation) is conducted at the end of the change effort or a change effort cycle, to determine the value of the change effort in comparison to other alternatives (will the change effort continue, be modified, be duplicated, or be terminated)
    a. Cost-benefit
    b. Cost-effect
    c. Cost-utility
    d. Cost-efficiency

Nonprofit agencies need to be aware of the need for submission of annual and other reports to funders, including assurances of meeting IRS/tax requirements.

Reassessment data are often used as the basis for "need" with a continuing or expanded effort. Needs assessment assists in looking for patterns and interrelationships among data collected, as previously noted. The evaluative data collected, compiled, and disseminated during reassessment, focus upon the **essential components** of evaluation:
    a. Inputs: needs, demands, constraints, resources (including time)
    b. Throughputs: assignments of resources, service delivery. Etc. (how effectively are things progressing?)
    c. Outputs: serviced populations (how are they doing?)
    d. Outcomes: results over time

Areas for Evaluation
1. Effort or activities: quantity and quality of change activities; reflects that something is being done but not necessarily accomplishing anything
2. Performance or outcomes: concerns improvements in quality of life of clients or targets or both as result of the change effort
3. Adequacy of performance: concerns relationship between outcomes and total need, as identified early in the change process; comparison of need satisfied by program to existing need
4. Efficiency (cost): makes judgments about ratio between inputs (resources) and outputs/outcomes (see p. 32 for efficiency formula examples)
5. Implementation (action plan) process: tries to understand how and why program does/does not work; formative evaluation identifies, measures, and assesses what happens as intervention is implemented
    a. Participant observation
    b. Diverse quantitative and qualitative methods
    c. Group methods, i.e. focus sessions

Data that can be gathered for Evaluation
1. Client perceptions
2. Third party (external evaluator) perceptions
3. Change agent perceptions
4. Hard, measurable data or information
5. Client satisfaction

Requirements
1. Input from participants

2. Reflection on meaning
3. Timing
4. Momentum
5. Readiness
6. Acceptance and approval
7. Closure

Reassessment: serves specific evaluative function – to determine overall success for planning "next" episode (to have or not to have)
1. How responsive are/were we to change?
2. Did we fulfill our objectives?
3. Were our designees and structure appropriate?
4. Do we have adequate resources to continue?
5. Were the consequences of implementation positive or negative?
6. What did our monitoring (formative evaluation) activities indicate? Could we handle this?
7. Was evaluation adequate?

Stabilization: targets the refinement of process
1. How do/can we integrate with other systems?
2. How do/can we routinize procedures?
3. How do/can we develop ongoing support?
4. What happens to the change agent?

Roles of the Change Agent:
1. Critic/reviewer
2. Facilitator
3. Advocate
4. Interpreter
5. "Closure"

Potential reassessment and stabilization issues:
1. Are you still credible as a change agent?
2. Do you have the energy to continue?
3. Is there still a need?
4. What does the planning team think?

Common Pitfalls:
1. Inflexibility
2. Intolerance for confusion
3. Poor group process
4. Inadequate communication
5. Lack of distributed leadership/ development of leadership among members
6. Lack of follow through on tasks
7. Turning fears into anger
8. Poor development efforts

TO DO!

#1 Develop reassessment and stabilization methods and establish criteria for your Change Effort.

_____
_____
_____
_____
_____

#2 Develop evaluative criteria and/or questions to assess the Change Agent's performance/role in the Change Effort.

_____
_____
_____

#3 Develop evaluative criteria and/or questions to assess the Team's performance/role in the Change Effort.

Key terms and Concepts: Can you define and explain each of the following key terms? Are you prepared to offer brief examples or applicable context for each concept?

Closure:

Change Letter:

Efficiency:

Etiology:

Inputs:

Momentum:

Outcomes:

Outputs:

Process Evaluation:

Reassessment:

Stabilization:

Throughputs:

_____

_____

Questions:

Identify and explain the components of evaluation.
What are common pitfalls in evaluation?

Chronicle and Rumination

This is the space provided to _CHRONICLE_ your thoughts and to _RUMINATE_ over the material presented in this chapter along with the references, outside readings, classroom activities, and experiences. Documenting your thoughts and feelings will provide a written account of your _Effective Planning Strategies and Proposal Writing_ education.

Appendix

Grant Resources

Federal Grants – These are the main websites for federal funding but not at all an exhaustive list.

http://www.grants.gov/ - Grants.gov a one stop website for all federal grants.
http://www.gpoaccess.gov/ - Federal Registry for laws and bills that drive grant funding.
http://www.hhs.gov/grants/ - Department of Health & Human Services
http://12.46.245.173/cfda/cfda.html - Catalog of Federal and Domestic Assistance – A database of federal grants that can be searched by topic or subject area.
http://www.firstgov.gov/ - First Gov - An all inclusive website for government grants and services.
http://www.ed.gov/index.jhtml - U.S. Department of Education
http://www.house.gov/ffr/resources_all.shtml - A resource for grants and grant writing.
http://www.hud.gov – Housing and Urban Development (HUD) – HUD gives out a lot of money in grants.

PA State Grant Resources – Again just a partial list of some main websites for PA

http://www.state.pa.us/ - Main PA state website where you can go to different departments depending on the focus of your grant.
http://www.newpa.com/ - PA Department of Community and Economic Development (DCED) – A good number of grants come from DCED. This is where the old WAM (Walking Around Money) is located now.
http://www.pde.state.pa.us/ - PA Department of Education – Resources for schools and community based programs.
http://www.pccd.state.pa.us/pccd/site/default.asp - PA Commission on Crime and Delinquency
http://www.dpw.state.pa.us/General/FormsPub/BlockGrants/ - PA Department of Public Welfare.
http://www.depweb.state.pa.us/dep/site/default.asp - Department of Environmental Protection.
http://www.dcnr.state.pa.us – Department of Parks and Recreations
Note: All states have similar sites.

Foundations

www.foundationcenter.org/ - The Foundation Center - This is the main website for foundation searches. They have a subscription-based service as well as some free stuff.
http://www.grantstation.com – The Grant Station – This is pretty much a paid service.
http://www.tgci.com/ - The Grantsmanship Center – These folks have excellent training resources and free grant resources on their website.
http://philanthropy.com/ – The Chronicle of Philanthropy – This is one of the biggie websites for fundraisers and includes some grant resources.
http://foundation.verizon.com/ - The Verizon Foundation gives a good bit of money for technology.
http://www.sbc.com/gen/corporate-citizenship?pid=7736 – The AT & T Foundation
http://www.neafoundation.org/grants.htm - National Education Association Foundation (NEA) – The is the teachers association foundation
www.schoolgrants.org
http://www.counseling.org
www.cwla.org/advocacy
www.k12grants.org
www.philantropy.com/grants

General Resources

www.census.gov/
www.npguides.org/
http://grants.nih.gov/grants/grant_tips.htm
http://www.socialedge.org/features/resources/support/how-to-write-grants/?searchterm=grants

Glossary of Terms

Action Plan - a specific outline or framework identifying a method of bringing about change or accomplishment

Advisory Board – an identified group of individuals selected to provide recommendations or guidance on a particular project

Assumption – a fact or statement taken for granted or given to be true

Assurances – the act or action of guaranteeing; also the instrument by which it is conveyed

Authoritative Evidence – quoting a recognized authority (individual, group, agency, or organization)

Boundaries of Competence - knowledge of skill level and level of expertise (certifications, licensees, training) and working within the limits/expectations of your skill level/expertise

Budget – a statement of the financial position of an administration for a defined period of time based on estimates of expenditures during the period and proposals for financing them; a plan for the coordination of resources and expenditures

Centile or Centile Points – provides the point on a scale below which a certain percentage of cases fall

Change Agent - individuals at the core of getting things done

Change Effort – when an idea is put to pen and paper and the work begins on the steps to address the opportunity

Change Episode – is the period of time for which the project or proposal is funded

Change Opportunity – the idea, before it is on paper

Child Protective Service Law – policy and procedure mandated for protection of abuse to minors

Cluster Sample – involve not selecting individuals, but rather using existing units. Not selecting all students but selecting specific schools from the total list

Code of Ethics - a set of guidelines and expectations concerning acceptable standards of professional behavior, unsupported by specific laws or governmental regulations

Combination change effort – usually project change effort/program change effort, where one effort begins and another is "built in" to take its place, later on, i.e. a stress management workshop is provided for a month; if all goes well, it will evolve into a regular part of service provision (this is an example of a project turned into a program design)

Continuous Recording – constant, uninterrupted documentation of a specified observable task or occurrence

Correlations – show the degree of relationship between two sets of measures

Criterion -- a standard on which a judgment or decision may be based

Descriptive Statistics – are used to describe a group of individuals which have been observed

Design – deliberate positive planning, a project or scheme in which

Dissemination Plan – how results of a change effort will be shared and with whom

Driving Forces – those who are in positions of power to ensure success

Duty to Warn – legal concept to protect

Etiology – reasons behind an existing condition

Evaluation Plan – used to review results ("success") of a change effort

Expressed Need – input from the target population; i.e. interviews, case studies, surveys

Facilitating Forces – those not directly responsible for your success but could have a negative impact if not included

Feasibility – whether or not a change effort is possible

Force-Field Analyses – reviews existing structure in order to maximize potential success

Formative Evaluation – monitoring the change effort during implementation

Fugitive literature – non-refereed journals; i.e. annual reports, public demographics (census), News Letters, On-line Publications, personal communications

Funding Cycle – period of time for which a change effort is funded

Funding Source – provider of funds

Gantt Chart – used to plot activities in outlining procedures for a change effort

Goals – visions that broadly direct a change effort

Inferential Statistics – (sampling statistics) are used to make inferences about the total population in terms of observed samples of the total population

Instrumentation –any measure/assessment used during the change effort

Leadership – method(s)/approaches used by those within an organization with authority to effect change

Likert Scale – weighted scaling used to determine strength of participant responses on a needs assessment

Mean Score– a measure of central tendency that identifies the average

Measures of Central Tendency – (mean, median, & mode) serve as reference points for interpreting scores

Measures of Dispersion or Validity - range and standard deviation

Mechanistic organizations – "typical" hierarchical, bureaucratic organizational systems

Median Score– a measure of central tendency that identified the middle score of a distribution

Methods – procedures used to implement a change effort

Mission Statement – purpose behind the development of an organization

Mode Score– a measure of central tendency that identified the most frequent score in a distribution

Need – substantiation of the necessity for a change effort

Needs Assessment – method used to operationalize substantiation of need

Normal Distribution Curve – the distribution of scores fall within the theoretical bell shaped curve

Objective – measurable target outcome of a change effort

Opportunity – description of what can be changed or effected, used instead of the word "problem", reflects a more positive position related to what needs changed

Organic Organizations – systems organized by role assignment based upon expertise

Organizational Chart – reflects organizational structure

Outcomes – evaluative results over time after change effort has concluded

Outputs – evaluative results immediately following a change effort

Perceived Need – survey/interview of the service providers of the target population; agency or organization or group rationale

Pilot Project – a trail project with the intent to continue funding for a program, if the pilot is successful

Planning Team – advisory group used to assist the Change Agent in substantiating need, etc. for a change effort

Policy change design/effort – change to existing organizational policy; i.e. changing organization through adding a position, changing personnel policy, changing curricula, etc.

Private Funders – foundations or individuals willing to support or contribute funds, usually have an agenda; follow trends identified by the board or chairmen

Project Director - overseeing role in a program; i.e. oversees the budget

Program design/change effort - lasting at least 6 months with provision of direct services to consumers

Project design/change effort – short-term (6 months or less) resembling program change; often used as a "pilot"

Proposal – planning document submitted for consideration (approval) to decision-makers

Public Funders – government or public monies (tax dollars), oriented towards social trends; i.e. National Institute of Health (NIH)

Range – the distance between the highest and lowest score

Rationale – justifies the reason for (need) the proposed initiative/change effort

Reassessment – serves specific evaluative function to determine overall success or failure

Relative Need – review of the literature including similar initiatives with comparisons of similar opportunities or programs

Release of Information—relates to informed consent

Reliability – consistency of measure, or freedom from measurement error

Researcher/Change Agent Bias – preconceived ideas that a researcher/change agent may have about outcomes that counter objectivity

Resource Plan – includes all resources necessary for a change effort to take place

Restraining forces – those that might try to hinder your success

Request for proposal – (RFP) - from a funding source, when there is money identified/allocated for projects of a specific type (these can be located on line or using the Federal Registry at the library)

Semi-Structured Interview – topics are specified in advance, but this approach provides flexibility in the sequence in which the topics are explored

Simple Random Selection – every individual in the population has an equal chance of being selected

Standard Deviation – the root mean square of the deviations from the mean

Standard Scores – a converted score based on a mean of zero and a standard deviation of one

Strategic planning – a formal process designed to help an organization identify and maintain an optimal alignment with the most important elements of its environment

Strategy – an agreed-upon course of action and direction that changes the relationship or maintains an alignment that helps to assure a more optimal relationship between the institution and its environment

Stratified Sample – individuals are selected for the norming group based on certain demographic characteristics (race, gender, socioeconomic level, amount of education, or religion)

Structured Interview – consists of prescribed questions that are asked in a prescribed sequence with little to no deviation

Stabilization – at the end of a change effort, this involves discussion of "what next", i.e. whether or not to continue

Summative Evaluation – evaluating results at the end of a change effort; may include follow-up

Survey- -instrument used to substantiate need within a planning document

SWOT Analysis – planning method that strategically analyzes strengths, weaknesses, opportunities and threats to a change effort

Target Population – specific group toward which an effort is directed

Theory – a set of concepts, laws, suppositions that describe and explain phenomena; enable the user to understand the underlying dynamics and make predictions

Throughputs – assignment of resources, service, delivery, etc; includes implementation components that must be monitored during a change effort.

Validity – the inferences that can be drawn from scores or other information obtained through an assessment

Bibliography

Cowher, S. (1997). A power development model for managing conflict. *Scholars, 6*(2), 24-27.

Cowher, S. (1996). A power development model for managing and preventing conflict. *Guidance and Counseling, 11*(4), 18-22.

Drummond, R., & Jones, K. (2006). *Assessment procedures for counselors and helping professionals.* Upper Saddle River, NJ: Pearson.

Fisher, R., & Ury, W. (1991). *Getting to yes.* New York: Penguin.

Fujishin, R. (1997). *The leader within.* San Francisco, CA: Acada.

George, J., & Cowan, J. (1999). *A handbook of techniques for formative evaluation.* Sterling, VA: Stylus.

Gitlin, L., & Lyons, K. (2004). *Successful grant writing.* New York: Springer.

Glanz, J. (2006). Fundamentals of educational research. Norwood, MA: Christopher-Gordon.

Glanz, J. (2002). Finding your leadership style: A guide for educators. Association for Supervision & Curriculum Development.

Glanz, J. (2000). Our natural life energies, explained. *Education Update, 42*(3), 5.

Glanz, J. (1994). Redefining the roles and responsibilities of assistant principals. *The Clearing House, 67*(5), 283-288.

Hagberg., J. (2003). *Real power.* Salem, WI: Sheffield.

Hall, G., & Hord, S. (2001). *Implementing change: Patterns, principles and potholes.* Boston, MA: Allyn and Bacon.

Homan, M. (2008). *Promoting community change.* Pacific Grove, CA: Brooks/Cole.

Homan, M. (1999). *Rules of the name: Lessons from the field of community change.* Pacific Grove, CA: Brooks/Cole.

Hulse-Killacky, D., Killacky, J., & Donigian, J. (2001). *Making task groups work in your world.* Upper Saddle River, NJ: Merrill.

Johnson, D., & Johnson, F. (2009). *Joining together.* Needham Heights, MA: Allyn and Bacon.

Kaplin, W, & Lee, B (2007). The law of higher education. San Francisco, CA: Jossey-Bass.

Kaufman, R., & Herman, J. (1991). *Strategic planning in education rethinking, restructuring, revitalizing.* Lancaster, PA: Technomic Publishing Company.

Null, G. (1996). *Who are you really? Understanding your life's energy.* New York: Carroll & Graf.

Peters, T., & Waterman, R. (1984). *In search of excellence.* New York: Warner.

Purkey, W., & Seigel, B. (2003). *Becoming an invitational leader.* Atlanta, GA: Humanics.

Stringer, E., & Dwyer, R. (2005). *Action research in human services.* Upper Saddle River, NJ: Pearson.

Weinhold, B., & Weinhold, J. (2000). *Conflict resolution: The partnership way.* Denver, CO: Love.

Wheeler, A., & Betram, B. (2008). *The counselor and the law.* Alexandria, VA: ACA.

Index of Terminology

About the Authors

Dr. Salene Cowher is a licensed professional counselor (LPC) who also holds national certification as a counselor (NCC), as well as school counseling and secondary English teaching certifications in Pennsylvania. She has been employed for the past 17 years as a counselor educator at Edinboro University of Pennsylvania and has maintained a private practice in Charlotte, North Carolina and Cambridge Springs, Pennsylvania. Prior to working at Edinboro, Dr. Cowher spent most of her career as a college counselor and administrator. She has also worked as a school counselor and public school teacher, specializing in working with at-risk adolescents.

Dr. Cowher earned her Ph.D. at University of Pittsburgh in 1984, where she concentrated in individual counseling and psychotherapy and program development. She earned an M.A. in guidance and counseling at Slippery Rock University of Pennsylvania in 1980 and a B.S. in secondary education English from Slippery Rock in 1975. She has written several funded grant proposals for programs focusing on rural youth, students with disabilities, and gender inequities. She has previously edited a planning text and authored a book on dreamwork and related techniques. Her published articles have included the topics of conflict management, self-esteem, psychosocial development, gender issues, post-traumatic stress disorder, and leadership.

Dr. Cowher lives in Cambridge Springs, PA with her husband, John. She is the proud mother of a son, Roderick, and grandmother to granddaughter, Gracelyn.

Larry S. Dickson is a licensed professional counselor (LPC) with national certification as a counselor (NCC) and international certifications as a Co-Occurring Disorders Professional Diplomate (CCDP) and a Certified Criminal Justice Professional (CCJP) Additionally he holds certification from the American Psychotherapy Association as a Certified Relationship Specialist (CRS) and holds an elementary education teaching certificate in Pennsylvania. He has been employed for the past 21 years in administrative positions in the mental health/mental retardation field. Larry has been employed as the Clinical Director of Bethesda Children's Home since 2004 and work in private practice in association with the Meadville Medical Center thought the Mind Body Wellness Center.

Larry earned a M.A. Degree in Rehabilitation Counseling from Edinboro University of Pennsylvania in 2003 and a B.A. in elementary education, early childhood and child development from Edinboro University of Pennsylvania in 1980. He developed several residential program descriptions that have been successfully licensed by the Department of Public Welfare and the Office of Mental Health.

Larry lives in Saegertown, PA with his wife, Margaret. Larry has three children: Bernie, Chad, and Sara and a granddaughter, Lizy.

32896772R00061

Made in the USA
Middletown, DE
08 January 2019